CONCERNING PRAYER

Mary Kathryn Pearce

STUDY GUIDE BY MAXINE WEST

General Board of Global Ministries

The United Methodist Church

CONCERNING PRAYER by Mary Kathryn Pearce
STUDY GUIDE by Maxine West

A publication of the Women's Division.
Produced by the General Board of Global Ministries
The United Methodist Church
475 Riverside Drive
New York, New York 10115

Printed in the United States of America
Library of Congress Catalog Card Number: 2004103545

Please address critiques or comments to:

Executive Secretary for Spiritual and Theological Development
Women's Division
General Board of Global Ministries, Room 1502
475 Riverside Drive
New York, NY 10115

ISBN #1890569-84-4

Contents

Preface

It was a cold and dreary November Friday when the call came for me to consider writing a study on prayer for Women's Division. What more could be written about prayer? I struggled with the request and then prayed. The heaviest and darkest clouds possible had been surrounding me for several months after the tragic death of someone who had faithfully modeled the Christian life for me. After the loss of such a faithful friend, it was prayer that had maintained my focus and expanded the peripheral vision of my heart. Pieces of Henri Nouwen's *The Wounded Healer* echoed in my mind for weeks. I turned again to loving God's people as if each were the only one, as Mother Teresa had instructed for years.

Could there be a way to explain some of the practical behaviors of people who had immersed their lives in prayer? How could such ways of living be defined and applied to the present: when cell phones are attached to ears; e-mail has made personal letters obsolete; time is defined as money; and few have little time to listen to another's life experiences?

It wasn't as if prayer was unfamiliar; prayer had been my spiritual diet for years. As a child, my faith developed in the church school at First United Methodist Church in Marshall, Illinois. My prayer life was planted by the faithful women and men who taught Sunday school, sang in the choirs, led youth groups, taught songs of faith, and always welcomed children.

They were diligent in swaddling many young lives in prayer. I and others were fortunate to receive such warmth. Could I write a study that would motivate those in our churches today to receive children of all ages and introduce them to the gift of prayer?

As a young adult, I followed a path to an area of southern Indiana that I have continually defined as at the heart of Methodism. I was surrounded by United Methodists, including a principal and faculty who welcomed me into their church. Within the first year, I discovered that prayer is contagious and that I had to be careful what I prayed for!

Remarkable people graced me with their prayers of empowerment. Wherever the path of prayer led, I was always in the presence of faithful United Methodist Women. I yearned to understand what the integral component was in Gene Maxwell's life as she struggled with cancer and still remained focused on sharing possibilities and faith with the women of the Korean UMC. Could a spiritual growth study on prayer incorporate a vision of embracing another in the midst of pain while living with unanswered prayers? What fed Gene's hope and what robbed others of hope in the presence of despair? Could I write a study that would inspire such integrity in one's relationships with God and others in order to live a life of prayer?

I took on the task of writing this spiritual growth study. I listened to the people who surround me as I serve them in the ministry of the church. I must acknowledge the faith-filled support of Judy Lowery and Nancy Varness, who have walked closely with me on this spiritual journey.

With the direction of the Holy Spirit in prayer, I have responded to my own and other questions in the pages that follow. As you turn the pages, I hope you will enfold your reading in a prayer for the Spirit of God to enlighten your journey. Please proceed with caution! Prayer is powerful and constant!

Introduction

Periodically, life has pushed me toward a deeper understanding of my relationship with God. Some of these powerful pushes have raised such questions as: Why was my prayer not answered? How could evil exist if God is listening? How many people have to pray before God hears?

In beginning to write this study, I asked children, young people, and adults around me, "What is prayer?" Their answers mostly came back as, "It's how we talk with God."

I discovered that many people are not aware that the Christian faith includes two major forms of prayer: active prayer (talking to God) and passive or dispositional prayer (listening to God). As in any relationship, regular, ongoing communication is necessary. Without it, relationships soon deteriorate. In many relationships, people focus on their own stories and needs. A common mistake with prayer is to do all the talking. Listening is essential if we regard prayer as communication.

I found that when I listened closely to God, I could hear people more clearly. It was at this "listening post" that my prayer life gained depth. The sounds of weeping, hungry children praying for food have haunted me. Angry prayers for social justice have stirred me. Wailing prayers that demand an explanation of pain have echoed in my heart. From mute to loud, prayers come from people in all situations.

Suffering always brings up the question of whether or not God answers prayers. Why do some prayers get answered while others do not?

The Scriptures encourage us to pray and believe that God will answer prayer. In John 15:4, I was comforted by knowing that power comes from abiding in him. What if I don't abide in him? Could my prayers still be answered? George Buttrick in his book *Prayer* reminds us of a familiar passage from a beloved novel—Huckleberry Finn's account of prayer:

> Miss Watson she took me in the closet and prayed, but nothing come of it. She told me to pray every day, and whatever I asked for I would get it. But it warn't so. I tried it. Once I got a fishline, but no hooks. It warn't any good to me without hooks. I tried for the hooks three or four times, but somehow I couldn't make it work. By and by, one day, I asked Miss Watson to try for me, but she said I was a fool. She never told me why, and I couldn't make it out no way. I set down one time back in the woods, and had a long think about it. I says to myself, if a body can get anything they pray for, why don't Deacon Winn get back the money he lost on pork? Why can't the widow get back her silver snuffbox that was stole? Why can't Miss Watson fat up? No, says I to myself, there ain't nothing in it.
> —Mark Twain, *The Adventures of Huckleberry Finn*

One can smile wistfully at this fine example of a child's thoughts about prayer. Yet I have heard adults say that it is no use asking God for anything. Some even conclude that there is no God to answer the prayer. But, when I return to my faith-base, the truth speaks again: there is a God who cares about all creation and seeks to be in a relationship with everyone. In a relationship, an infinite number of events and dynamics are possible. When we commit to any relationship, we must be present, bring our full selves, and be willing to learn and grow. In prayer, we are present to God and God is present to us. The results of such encounters are infinite. My task is to deepen this relationship in the time I am given to live my life.

Though there are a variety of methods and definitions of prayer, for the purpose of this study, the following prayer definitions will be used.

Invocation—the intentional reminding of oneself that God is present, the awareness of the Divine presence. It is the act of inviting God to bring the awareness of Spirit into one's mind and soul. To paraphrase Tennyson, God is closer to us than breathing and nearer than hands and feet. Wherever one is, so is God.

Confession—the honest telling of one's sins and mistakes to God; to be honestly sorry and sincerely to request forgiveness. There are two aspects necessary for confession: in-depth self-examination and the application of integrity to self. "If we confess our sins, God is faithful and just to forgive us our sins, and to cleanse us from all unrighteousness." (1 John 1:9) With this gift of forgiveness comes the responsibility to accept the challenge to be transformed and alter the behavior that created the sin.

Thanksgiving—the result of a grateful heart. Gratitude gathers force in the soul and becomes a geyser of affirming faith. There are four reasons for thanksgiving: Jesus Christ; all the means of grace, the great joys and wonders of life; the gifts one receives; and people in our lives.

Petition—the part of prayer that asks God for what is needed for living. This prayer arises from the realization that one is neither omniscient nor omnipotent. Intensity increases within the soul to offer up one's hopes and dreams to this greater Being. Petition is also asking God to give what is best. At a critical time in my life, a beloved spiritual mentor gave me a question to ask myself during prayer: Is my need clearly something that holds my heart?

Intercession—lifting the needs of the world to God and asking for blessing and help. The naming of those in need is critical. Many stories reveal the power of intercessory prayer, but one of the most amazing comes from St. Augustine's life. His mother, Monica, exercised unceasing prayer for her son. In the *Confessions*, written about A.D. 400, Augustine emphasizes the influential and strenuous prayer life of his mother. She prayed night and day that he might discover Christianity; she prayed by herself in her own home, for her husband did not share her faith; she prayed with others within her community of faith; and she had an audience with her bishop, who shared her concerns.

Despite not knowing when God's response would come, she did not stop believing that God would respond. She did receive an essential truth: intercessory prayer at this level changes the one doing the praying. Selfish desires and self-centered anxieties are soon forgotten;

thoughts, attitudes, and actions mobilize to a new center. One begins to see others with new eyes and enjoys an ever-evolving community of fellowship. Ultimately, Monica became a newborn change-agent of God's work. Her heart vision became clearer, the better to see what she could do to influence her son.

In the depth of Augustine's being, he knew that, wherever he was, his mother was praying for him. His heart was humbled. Knowing that someone is praying for you strengthens you in moments of doubt, comforts you in need, and opens up possibilities.

Christ-like intercession is one of the most intense ways to commune with God. The Christian intercessor grows increasingly unselfish, losing oneself to the love of God and the love of others. The intercessor stands at God's side, enlisted for the task of redeeming others.

Theresa of Avila, a master of intercessory prayer, said: "Those who walk in the way of prayer have the greater need of learning; and the more spiritual they are, the greater is their need." The more we pray, the more we need to know.

I prayerfully invite you to deepen your knowledge of prayer and to discover your new spiritual awareness. Throughout the journey, please remember that all things are possible!

PRAYER

Jesus prayed and instructed his disciples to pray. We who have responded to the call to be his disciples must put prayer at the center of our being. An old but familiar hymn, "Prayer Is the Soul's Sincere Desire" (1818),[1] gives a working definition of prayer and a context from which to begin our journey.

> Prayer is the soul's sincere desire,
> unuttered or expressed,
> the motion of a hidden fire
> that trembles in the breast. *(verse 1)*

These words by James Montgomery define prayer as knowing one's soul. Life is an awakening through each moment that the soul seeks to be with another. For the spiritually hungry, this seeking ultimately reveals God and is always in a state of growth and transformation.

The expressions of the soul are infinite: a violin, a voice, a canvas, etc. During these powerful expressions, prayer rises and a "link" is established. God is present as we affirm our relationship with God.

> Prayer is the burden of a sigh,
> the falling of a tear,
> the upward glancing of an eye,
> when none but God is near. *(verse 2)*

A variety of acronyms remind us to pray: ASAP—always say a prayer; PUSH—pray until something happens; FROG—fully rely on God. Others explain the act of prayer: PRAYER—psalming, reconciling, adoring, yielding, entreating, realizing[2]; PRAY—praise, repent, ask (for others), yourself.

As a pastor, I have often observed a spiritual gathering sink to puzzlement when I ask someone to close with prayer! "Oh, I can't do that! I don't pray out loud." "I'm not comfortable in praying." What is it that keeps so many of us from sharing the words in our souls? Our baptism has anointed us with the grace to extend ourselves in prayer to God.

I believe, along with those who have gone before—Jochebed, Moses, Miriam, Abraham, Hagar, Joshua, Rahab, David, Deborah, Isaiah, Elizabeth, Jesus, the bent-over-woman, the blind man, Lydia, Paul, Priscilla, James, Phoebe, Martin Luther, Susanna Wesley, John Wesley—that prayer is about coming to the very center of life. Teilhard de Chardin defined it as "the center of centers."[3] It is the opening and offering of the mind, heart, and soul in a continual conversation with God. Sometimes the conversation is anointed with tears or with a silent flow of joy. But the conversation never really ends.

> Prayer is the simplest form of speech
> that infant lips can try;
> prayer the sublimest strains that reach
> the Majesty on high. *(verse 3)*

Prayer is the turning of life God-ward and is not limited to just words. One's thoughts and deeds speak prayers as well. Prayer is a living out of faith. Prayer becomes action when a person values a gift God has given, and claims the responsibility that goes with it.

There is an ever-growing market for spirituality in the global community today. People report that they are hungry to have more than knowledge about God; they are seeking a relationship. Many of them begin the arduous process of seeking and searching only to feel that spirituality eludes them. Jesus said: "I do not give as the world gives. Do not let your hearts be troubled. Do not be afraid. My peace I give to you." (John 14:27) We yearn for that peace—the inward music of the soul singing the melodies of hope, forgiveness, and a radiating glory.

One does not pray from a well gone dry, but from an eternal spring always gushing forth. One prays not because God is distant but because of God's closeness. One prays not because of what is needed but because of all one has. From the biblical perspective, the desire to pray flows from a need to be a mirror reflecting the glory and grace of God.

Jeremiah is an example of one who eagerly sought an intimate communion with Yahweh (Jeremiah 10:23f; 12:1-4; 15:15-18; 20:7-11). He viewed this relationship as a reward for the affliction he had endured. He suffered when the relationship was not going well.

The Deuteronomic code required that love for God be expressed in spiritual devotion. After 587 B.C., the emphasis increased because of the destruction of the Temple. The holy place—the physical link—was gone. Prayer became the means to accomplish worship. "My flesh and my heart may fail, but God is the strength of my heart and my portion for ever." (Psalm 73:26)

> Prayer is the contrite sinners' voice,
> returning from their way,
> while angels in their songs rejoice
> and cry, "Behold, they pray!" *(verse 4)*

The disciple approached Jesus and wanted to know how to pray. The response became known as the Lord's Prayer (Matthew 6:9-13; Luke 11:2-4). If one looks closely at this model, one finds that praying is not about receiving but about offering—offering expressions that reveal God's glory and strength. Jesus defines the priority of prayer as seeking first the kingdom and then righteousness. The Lord's Prayer contains only one material request—our daily bread. The prayer is God-centered, offering servanthood.

Praying is similar to writing. One can look at a computer screen or a piece of paper forever and have nothing to say. Until one plunges in, there is no beginning, just stagnation. I used to remind high school composition students that the longer they sit and wait for inspiration, the more brain cells would die. Stagnation breeds stagnation. This is what happens when a person says that he or she cannot pray. William James had a great answer for that problem: The reason why we pray is simply that we cannot keep from praying.[4]

Many times prayer begins with petition: I need this, God. Give me strength, God. And then it moves to bargaining: If you help me pass the test just this once, God, I promise I'll study for the next one. One's prayer life, though, must develop toward maturity. So, in the end, we can pray like Jesus, "not my will but yours be done." (Luke 22:42).

When one turns to prayer, there is an empowerment that comes into the soul and enables one more fully to participate in creation. From wonder to disappointment and pain, our expressions show the presence of God. Prayer happens! Are we able to recognize what is happening around us? Are we aware of being one with God?

All life is interrelated. Jesus said: "Abide in me as I abide in you. Just as the branch cannot bear fruit by itself unless it abides in the vine, neither can you unless you abide in me. I am the vine; you are the branches. Those who abide in me and I in them bear much fruit, because apart from me you can do nothing." (John 15:4-5) As individuals, we are unique; but all of life is intertwined. Beyond all human relationships is the relationship to God, who yearns for wholeness and holiness. Prayer is the means by which companionship with God is deepened.

Jesus demonstrated his relationship with God as a living prayer. In all of his teachings, healings, and sacrifice, he leaned deeply upon his inward and personal relationship with God. He went away from the crowds in order to be alone, to ponder, to commune, to pray. In the Garden of Gethsemane he revealed the deepest struggle and most painful utterances of his soul as he again defined his relationship with God. His life, girded in prayer, reveals inner strength and outward confidence because he walked with God in trust and hope.

Jesus came from a people who knew this routine. In Israel, prayer was a fixed pattern in the religious life of the people, a discipline begun in youth. In Deuteronomy 6:4-7, we see the foundation for a life of prayer:

> "Hear, O Israel: The Lord our God is one Lord; and you shall love the Lord your God with all your heart, and with all your soul, and with all your might. And these words which I command you today shall be upon your heart; and you shall teach them diligently to your children,

and shall talk of them when you sit in your house, and when you walk by the way, and when you lie down, and when you rise."

This creed, surrounded by benedictions, was known as the Shema (pronounced *sheh-máh*). Reciting it twice a day was the minimum requirement. These words were the beginning of any child's understanding of religious practice. It became the custom to begin and end each day with this recitation.[5]

Other customs would have been part of Jesus' upbringing. In Daniel 6:10-13, we see Daniel kneeling before, praising, and praying to God three times each day. The afternoon prayer took place at 3:00 p.m. in the Temple, and the community would gather there. At this time the daily sacrifice was offered in the Temple. During the three hours of prayer, the Tefilla (pronounced *t'feeLA*)—a hymn consisting of a string of benedictions—was prayed. Those who prayed this hymn would add their own private petitions. Only those who were considered "free men were obliged to recite the Shema, whereas the Tefilla was to be said by all, including women, children, and even slaves."[6]

In Acts 3:1; 10:3, 30, the custom of praying three times a day had become part of the regular ritual. The two customs—reciting the Shema twice a day and praying three times a day—were blended thus: in the morning, the devout Jew would say the Shema and the Tefilla together; in the afternoon only the Tefilla (called the hour of prayer); in the evening, the Shema and the Tefilla.

For Jews in the New Testament, sunrise, sunset, and 3:00 p.m. were the daily times of prayer. These three occasions of prayer, with the benedictions recited before and after meals, served as the framework for the practice of prayer for everyone. From a cultural perspective, Jesus was immersed in a life of prayer and reared in a devout home (Luke 2 and 4:16). He would have learned the prayers of his people as a child and attended Sabbath worship. In Mark 1:35, Jesus prayed before sunrise.

After the Feeding of the Five Thousand, Jesus ascends a mountain in the evening to pray (Mark 6:46), and when Luke relates that Jesus

5

continued all night in prayer before the choosing of the twelve apostles.... This is evidently the evening prayer which he has extended till dawn.[7]

The rhythm of praying three times each day gave him an internal source from which to draw his strength.

Mark 1:35—"And in the morning, rising up a great while before day, he went out, and departed into a solitary place."

Mark 6:46—"And when he had sent them away he departed into a mountain to pray."

Luke 6:12—"He went up into a mountain to pray, and continued all night in prayer to God."

He went beyond tradition by praying in his native tongue— Aramaic. He referred to God as "Abba." He gave his disciples a formal prayer in the vernacular when he taught them the Lord's Prayer. He took prayer from the liturgical domain and placed it in day-to-day life. Jesus removed the restrictions regarding who could pray, when to pray, and how to pray. He embraced the Spirit of God in all times and places.[8]

There are not many prayers by Jesus in the Gospels. In the Synoptic Gospels and apart from the crucifixion, there are only two prayers of Jesus. There is the cry of jubilation (Matthew 11:25) and the prayer in Gethsemane (Mark 14:36). The Gospel of John adds the following: the prayer in the story of Lazarus (11:41); a short prayer in the Temple outer court (12:27); and the high priestly prayer (17). There are other references made to Jesus praying. These "unknown prayers" of Jesus may be seen in the context of Mark 1:35, Matthew 14:22-23, Luke 5:15-16, Luke 6:12, Luke 9:28-29, and Luke 9:18.

Many of these were prayers of solitude and communion with the Spirit, a type of praying present throughout the history of Christianity. Others have sometimes taken them in different directions, but always seeking the companionship of the Spirit.

Prayer is the Christians' vital breath,
the Christians' native air;
their watch-word at the gates of death;
they enter heaven with prayer." *(verse 5)*

"Pondering," or meditation, nurtures a prayer-filled life. The biblical verb to *ponder* requires one to retreat from the business of daily life. It involves solitude and honest self-confrontation, which prepares one for the highest levels of prayer. Here one experiences absolute honesty with God, embraces the need for forgiveness, and seeks deeper understanding. Meditation, pondering, centering—all point to the rest that comes from knowing God as companion in life and death. Prayer develops empathy and caring about all of life.

Even Jesus, however, could not stay in the wilderness or on the Mount of Transfiguration. Real life calls us back from breathing God's Spirit. How does one keep exuberant the inner life of the soul while addressing all that life delivers? How can one live in the global community and be a person with a devout prayer life?

One of my earlier visits to the United Nations resulted in my yearning to know more about Dag Hammarskjold. Though he lived in a different time, one of his statements addresses today's seeker of spirituality.

I found in the writings of those great medieval mystics [that] "self-surrender" had been the way to self-realization, and … in "singleness of mind" and "inwardness" [they] had found strength to say yes to every demand, which the needs of their neighbors made them face….[9]

Life needs to be held in balance. Communing with God moves one to a life of giving.

O Thou, by whom we come to God,
the Life, the Truth, the Way:
the path of prayer thyself hast trod;
Lord, teach us how to pray! *(verse 6)*

The histories of the people of faith all reveal a standard theme: Alone, I was empty; I sought community with God and found the Spirit. The journey begins with one step.

EMBRACING A LIFE OF PRAYER

Imagine being present among those disciples who asked Jesus how to pray. The empire always reminds you of your low place in society; tradition calls you to be encircled with religiosity; you try to survive under emperors and economic crises; and you long for peace in your soul. Now this man—Jesus of Nazareth—continually speaks about a relationship with the "Father." Anxiety would have been stirring among those who hungered for more. The scene was one of great need and high expectation. With no hesitancy, Peter demands, "Lord, teach us how to pray." (Luke 11:1)

Often the need to pray becomes apparent when people see that life is out of their control. Sometimes it comes when nothing else seems to be happening and life stagnates. Sometimes it bursts forth with inspiration into the "Hallelujah Chorus." Ultimately, for most of us, a life of prayer begins when the soul opens up and reveals a void. There is incompleteness and a yearning for a presence that nothing else can fulfill.

Today's Western world is built on an economy based on concentrating solely on what is best for self. Western culture and media tell me over and over that I come first in this world.

This "me first" culture sometimes reduces decisions in United Methodist contexts to arguments about the cost of a ministry rather than discussions of creative ways to meet needs. Local churches where I have served have had to face the question: "What causes us to do or not do certain ministries?" Sometimes we forget to pray about our dilemma. Like Peter, we realize there must be more. Therefore, Lord, teach us to pray!

Just look at that last sentence. Peter's outburst shows us that even asking to learn how to pray establishes a relationship with our Lord and begins our life of prayer. The theologian Sören Kierkegaard defined praying thus: "If you don't breathe, you die. If you don't pray, you die spiritually."[10]

I have all too often been the pastor for persons who struggle with breathing problems. Whether caused by influenza, asthma, emphysema, or other respiratory diseases, there is no greater fear than not being able to get one's breath. In the midst of intense anxiety, it becomes very difficult to convince someone to relax, to breathe through the nose instead of the mouth, and to calm oneself. I recall an emergency room physician asking me to enter the exam cubicle to calm a parishioner. The physician said, "I can't get him to listen to me. I cannot get him to relax, to calm down. Maybe he will listen to you." How similar in tone and thought such an expression might be from the Great Physician. Now, just breathe deeply and exhale slowly; we are on a journey that will change life.

One form of prayer reflects the life-giving importance of breathing. The breath prayer involves breathing in a slow and deliberate rhythm that moves one from self-absorption to inhaling the breath or Spirit of God. Like the breath of God entering and flowing through one's being, oxygen saturates the entire body. An intriguing aspect of this kind of prayer is that exhaled breath is mostly water and carbon dioxide. And just as the breath we exhale cleanses us and helps plants to grow, so the Spirit of God cleanses us and transforms the world. Our survival depends on prayer as well as oxygen.

"Whether you like it or not, read and pray daily. It is for your life; there is no other way: else you will be a trifler all your days.... Do justice to your own soul; give it time and means to grow. Do not starve yourself any longer."[11] Even 300 years after John Wesley's birth, his words remain vital in understanding the effect of praying. As the hymn, "Near to the Heart of God," says, as one continues to move closer to the heart of God, there is a place of quiet rest, a place of comfort sweet, a place where all is joy and peace.

Teresa of Avila discovered at the age of 39 that to experience the Spirit of God at the center of her soul, she had to be in complete solitude. "[Her] discussions on prayer do not concern recited prayers, although she and the other nuns in the unreformed Carmelite Order to which she initially belonged were required to recite lengthy public prayers each day. Part of these daily recitations was composed from the psalms of the Bible."[12]

Her "mental prayer" was not based on words. "In fact, one of the progressive characteristics of mental prayer, a quality which grows in strength and pervasiveness as a person advances in prayer, is a receptiveness that is very still." This meant progressing toward the innermost dwellings of the soul, where one could be close to God. "Teresa is famous for her saying how hard it is to teach mental prayer to intellectuals. They always want to think."

> But returning to those who practice discursive reflection, I saw they should not pass the whole time thinking. For, although discursive reflection is very meritorious, they don't seem to realize that since their prayer is delightful there should ever be a Sunday or a time in which one is not working; but they think such time is lost. I consider this loss a great gain. But, as I have said, they should put themselves in the presence of Christ, and, without tiring the intellect, speak with and delight in Him and not wear themselves out in composing syllogisms; rather, they should show Him their needs and the reason why He doesn't have to allow us to be in His presence. The discursive reflection they can do at one time, and the other acts at another, so that the soul may not grow tired of always eating the same food. These acts are very delightful and helpful if one's taste becomes accustomed to them. They contain a great amount of sustenance giving the soul life and many benefits.[13]

In prayer, holiness becomes wholeness. Life becomes much simpler. One does not need to make demands on God. Striving to succeed by worldly standards becomes irrelevant, since it means being untrue to the deepest reflection of the soul.

An excellent biblical glimpse of prayer is the story of Mary, Martha, and Jesus:

> Now as they went on their way, he entered a village; and a woman named Martha received him into her house. And she had a sister

called Mary, who sat at the Lord's feet and listened to his teaching. But Martha was distracted with much serving; and she went to him and said, "Lord, do you not care that my sister has left me to serve alone? Tell her then to help me." But the Lord answered her, "Martha, Martha, you are anxious and troubled about many things; one thing is needful, Mary has chosen the good portion, which shall not be taken away from her." (Luke 10:38-42)[14]

Teresa viewed Martha's concerns as the rational activity of the mind and body. But to commune with the Lord requires quiet and solitude. Two one-hour periods each day for mental prayer revealed the presence of God. She felt a new willingness to follow God's voice.

William Shakespeare titled a play that brings to mind the mental busyness in which many of us in the United States have come to believe we must participate. The play is *Much Ado about Nothing*. Teresa of Avila would remind us to pray in stillness. Complete stillness, the stillness required to listen fully to another, is very challenging. Many of us schedule our lives so that there is never a quiet moment to listen to our own heart or the heart of another. How intentional are we in moving into the deepest dwellings of our souls and listening in absolute stillness to the Spirit of God?

The tapestry that Teresa wove in her life of prayer contains two primary colors: the color of determination and the color of humility. Her determination to heed the inner voice was coupled to a humility that enabled God to lift her soul.

"Not only is prayer the chief thing for which St. Teresa of Avila is known, it is at the heart of her identity as a person. It was prayer that brought Teresa out of the terrible decade of her twenties. Prayer was a central means whereby she overcame the paralysis of her own guilt and its accompanying compulsive perfectionism. It was prayer that was the chief means by which she learned to love her friends rather than just being in love with the feelings that accompany friendship.... Prayer was as much a part of her future life of action as it was in a more modern exemplar, Mohandas Gandhi. Teresa might well have used these words of Gandhi with respect to prayer:"

Prayer has saved my life. Without it, I should have been a lunatic long ago. I had my share of the bitterest public and private experiences. They threw me in temporary despair. If I was able to get rid of that despair, it was because of prayer…. It came out of sheer necessity, as I found myself in a plight where I could not possibly be happy without it. And as time went on, my faith in God increased, and more irresistible became the yearning for prayer. Life seemed to be dull and vacant without it…. I have found people who envy my peace. That peace comes from prayer. I am indifferent to the form. Everyone is a law unto himself in that respect. But there are some well-marked roads, and it is safe to walk along the beaten tracks trodden by the ancient teachers. I have given my personal testimony. Let every one try and find that as a result of daily prayer he adds something new to his life.[15]

To fill an empty life and improve spiritual health, refer to Teresa of Avila's understanding of prayer. Four categories would change in one's life with prayer: a) prayer helps one move from mundane noisiness to a depth within oneself; b) prayer gives greater emphasis to being rather than doing—one grows into a loving person through prayer; c) prayer solidifies union with God; the closer one is, the more loving one becomes; d) prayer is not an exit from life but provides confidence to meet what life brings.[16]

When one finally reaches this depth of prayer, there is a peace that truly passes all understanding.

The Middle Ages gave birth to another great woman of prayer, Hildegard of Bingen. It has been suggested that her life was significantly impacted by her frequent illnesses and visions and the decision of her parents to tithe her to God (she was their tenth child).

At the age of eight, she went to a Benedictine monastery to be educated. This monastery was Celtic in tradition and included women. At 18 she became a nun, and at 38 she was appointed abbess, head of the female community at the monastery. In medieval life, spirituality was the only path in which women could obtain leadership. Following this path, women could educate themselves through the monastic library. Hildegard invested her energies in learning as much as possible, including music, the sciences, and other disciplines.[17]

During the next four years, a series of visions changed her life. Hildegard used the image of light to describe her spiritual awakening:

> When I was forty-two years and seven months old, Heaven was opened and a fiery light of exceeding brilliance came and permeated my whole brain, and inflamed my whole heart and my whole breast, not like a burning but like a warming flame, as the sun warms everything its rays touch.[18]

Shortly after this, Hildegard received a vision that she interpreted as the call to preach and teach: "All of a sudden, I was able to taste of the understanding of the narration of books. I saw the Psalter clearly and the evangelists and other catholic books of the Old and New Testaments."[19]

This vision and others frightened her, and she hibernated in her sick bed. The fear subsided when she began to write about the visions and integrate their meaning into her life. She had withheld her visions for fear of retribution from the Church. Women were not allowed to preach; they were taught to be silent and humble if they intended to please God. It is understandable why Hildegard persistently portrayed herself as a weak, unlearned creature, a simple vessel of God.

With the vision to preach and teach, she realized that she would need the support of another, the monk Volmar. Volmar was her scribe, writing volume after volume during the next ten years. Hildegard often added drawings to help intepret the meaning of the visions.

But a woman who had such visions was considered suspicious. Pope Eugenius III sent a commission to investigate her work. The power and substance of her visions were not to be denied. The Pope's emissaries determined that her teaching and insights were accurate and recommended their approval by the Pope. Upon receiving approval from the Pope, she took the opportunity to ask that he work more diligently for Church reform.

Hildegard's visions were illuminations from the Holy Spirit. As at Pentecost (which Hildegard drew in her self-portrait), the tongues of fire that enabled communication awakened her. She alluded to the Holy Spirit as fire:

O Holy Spirit, Fiery Comforter Spirit, Life of the life of all crea-tures.... Who is the Holy Spirit?... The Holy Spirit is a Burning Spirit. It kindles the hearts of humankind.... The Holy Spirit resur-rects and awakens everything that is.[20]

She accepts the call to speak and set ablaze the hearts of people with compassion. Her illuminations rescue divinity from obscurity and free spirit-filled hearts to flow without ceasing into the rivers of life. The biblical prophets, Daniel and Ezekiel, strengthened her fortitude to claim her own prophetic role in the life of God's people. Whereas the common understanding was for a prophet to foretell the future, her claim was that she was called to criticize the present and thereby change the future in order to enhance the Kingdom of God.

Hildegard acknowledged the Spirit of God as a creative force call-ing her out of herself through music and poetry. She authored books on medical and pharmaceutical advice, a commentary on the Gospels, and three books on theology—integrating her visions with an understand-ing of God in her life. She also wrote an interdisciplinary study of the sciences, art, and religion. Perhaps her visionary language has been the greatest contribution toward establishing a global understanding of Christianity. Her themes were social justice, the downtrodden, claim-ing the image of God in each human being, and developing people's God-given gifts. From her *Book of Divine Works*, one can begin fully to embrace her life of prayer by praying her "Kyrie":

Creator God, draw compassion from us.
Christ, draw compassion from us.
Spirit God, draw compassion from us.[21]

A key person of prayer for United Methodists is, of course, John Wesley. Wesley knew he had been called to preach. His experience did not include illuminations or visions. Within his soul burned a truth that had to be communicated to all persons: This earthly life is temporary, and in the time it is granted, one must strive to attain Christian perfection—nothing less than union with God.[22] Christian perfection is embodied love, totally loving God and loving one's neighbor as oneself. Obtaining perfection equals giving to God one's soul, body, and substance. It means freeing oneself from all self-will, denying and resigning oneself completely to the will of God, praying earnestly, fasting, gradually dying to sin, and renewing oneself in the image of God. There could be no "half Christian" to Wesley. This kind of perfection requires us to give all we have, all we are.

[Wesley] was a descendant of several generations of Dissenting clerics with strong Puritan impulses; his father, Samuel Wesley, was a minister in the Church of England, and an interest in mystical writers extended back into his family for several generations. In his father's rectory in Epworth, Lincolnshire, John was taught to be a serious Christian, learning from his mother Susanna that "Religion is not confined to the church, or closet, nor exercised only in prayer and meditation. Everywhere we are in the presence of God, and every word and action is capable of morality."[23]

Like Hildegard, he discovered the mystical power that comes "where two or three are gathered in my name" (Matthew 18:20). While at Oxford, Wesley gathered believers and initiated praying together, studying Scripture, and encouraging one another to be intentional in living a moral life. Fasting was of critical significance—freeing oneself of all that might pull the mind, heart, and soul from communion with God. He discovered what others had who had come before him: when one is no longer self-absorbed, there is oneness with God. With the presence of God comes an inner desire to care for one's neighbor; Wesley developed a strong sense of social action. In caring for others, he saw the necessity of limiting his own expenses as much as he could. His passion was for holiness and a constant imitation of Christ; his energy for accomplishing his passion was grace.

Wesley embraced prayer and other activities as a means of grace.

His diaries reveal that for nearly 66 years, prayer was at the center of his heart. He daily noted time spent in prayer. For example, on Wednesday, February 24, 1791, he wrote: "4:45 prayed.... 6:30 prayed.... 2:00 prayed.... 9:30 prayed.[24] This entry was dated six days before his death. He preferred to say that he prayed with the Spirit directing him. For him, prayer was the desire of the soul articulated in words. He was confident "that the end of one's praying was not to inform God, as though God knows not your wants already, but rather to inform oneself; to fix the sense of those wants more deeply in your hearts, and the sense of your continual dependence on God who only is able to supply all your wants."

Simple expression mattered most to Wesley; one had only to wrap a need in prayer with the understanding that God's will would be done. People needed discipline in building a relationship with God and a fixed time daily for prayer. Furthermore, he broke with traditional mystics by discouraging mental prayer. He believed that "prayer almost always meant vocal prayer.... It is therefore our wisdom to force ourselves to prayer—to pray, whether we can pray or not. And many times while we are so doing, the fire will fall from heaven and we shall know our labour was not in vain."[25]

David A. DeSilva's book *Praying with John Wesley* is a guide to spiritual discipline using Wesley's format.

In 1733 John Wesley compiled "A Collection of Forms of Prayer for Every Day of the Week" for his own use and for others who sought a spiritual discipline by which to grow in virtue, in service, and into the image of Christ.

...

Wesley's forms for daily prayer seek to nurture six virtues that he considered indispensable for Christian discipleship. These are love for God, love for neighbor, humility, mortification, resignation, and gratitude. Morning and evening prayers provide a means for growth in each virtue. The morning devotion introduces the participant to the virtue that is to be the focus for that day. The evening devotion begins with a period of self-examination in which the participant reflects on the extent to which he or she has grown in that virtue during the day. The evening prayer provides an opportunity to ask again for God's help in making the day's virtue one's own.[26]

In "Minutes of Several Conversations," Wesley defines the instituted means of grace.

(1) Prayer; private, family, public; consisting of deprecation, petition, intercession, and thanksgiving. Do you use each of these? Do you use private prayer every morning and evening? If you can, at five in the evening; and the hour before or after morning preaching? Do you forecast daily, wherever you are, how to secure these hours? Do you avow it everywhere? Do you ask everywhere, "Have you family prayer?"[27]

Wesley knew his leaders would be empty if they did not practice the discipline of prayer. In "To the Societies at Bristol," he wrote:

To the public, constantly add the private means of grace, particularly prayer and reading. Most of you have been greatly wanting in this; and without this you can never grow in grace. You may as well expect a child to grow without food as a soul without prayer; and reading is an excellent help to this.[28]

John Wesley's life of prayer was a way to live in the presence of Christ. In every thought, word, and deed, he offered all to the Spirit of God and asked for the grace "to do all by the one who is within me."

Wesley's Covenant Prayer powerfully expresses his Christian commitment:

I am no longer my own, but thine. Put me to what thou wilt, rank me with whom thou wilt. Put me to doing, put me to suffering. Let me be employed by thee or laid aside for thee, exalted for thee or brought low by thee. Let me be full, let me be empty. Let me have all things, let me have nothing. I freely and heartily yield all things to thy pleasure and disposal. And now, O glorious and blessed God, Father, Son, and Holy Spirit, thou art mine, and I am thine. So be it. And the covenant which I have made on earth, let it be ratified in heaven. Amen.

Throughout the history of the church, many others have pondered union with God, listening for a lifetime to the voice of love. In the 20th century, Dietrich Bonhoeffer embraced this union as he struggled against the Nazis. At an early age, he declared that he wanted to become a pastor. He began his theological studies at Tuebingen and completed them at the University of Berlin. But no school had as much impact on his theology as the cell of a prison camp in Germany during World War II. His writings help others understand the presence of God in a world filled with hatred and destruction. Bonhoeffer, like so many others persecuted for their faith, was firmly committed to deepening his union with God regardless of the threat to his life.[29]

Bonhoeffer raised the question in prison: Why does it so often take a crisis to move people to pray when the Bible prescribes it as routine behavior? When intellectual stagnation appears to be stronger than faith, Bonhoeffer reminds one that it is then the time to pray. He concluded that one need not have a strong foundation of faith before embarking on a prayer life; just pray. My own observation of people who find prayer useless shows that the stronger one thinks one is, the harder one falls when the shallow foundation crumbles.

Through prayer, Bonhoeffer found strength "where two or three are gathered." His close friend Eberhard Bethge covenanted with him to be in prayer for the other. The commitment deepened and sustained them when Bonhoeffer was imprisoned for conspiring to assassinate Hitler and Bethge was in the German military. Bonhoeffer to Bethge:

Let us promise to remain faithful in interceding for each other.... And if it should be decided that we are not to meet again, let us remember each other to the end in thankfulness and forgiveness, and may God grant us that one day we may stand before his throne praying for each other and joining in praise and thankfulness.[30]

This handwritten note contains the power of a covenant wrapped in prayer and immersed in life. Bethge was able to pay Bonhoeffer two one-day visits, and that was all. Bonhoeffer was executed just days before the overthrow of the Nazi government.

Bonhoeffer made a point to extend himself to others; it didn't matter if the other was not a member of the Christian community. What did matter was the responsibility to be a Christian example to all. He gave of himself as pastor to his fellow prisoners. As others attested, he mirrored unflagging Christian hope and strength to the many who were hopeless. A friend and fellow resistance worker, Fabian von Schlabrendorff, was in the cell adjoining Bonhoeffer's during his last months in prison. He said:

> Outwardly, he [Bonhoeffer] betrayed no sign of what he had gone through: he was always in good spirits, always pleasant and considerate to everyone—so much so, in fact, that very soon and to my complete amazement even our guards fell under the spell of his personality.... As far as our relationship was concerned, he was always the hopeful one. He never tired of pointing out that the fight is lost only when you yourself give up. Often he would smuggle a scrap of paper into my hands on which he had written words of comfort or hope from the Bible.... To the very end, even in those dark days when the Nazi rule was crumbling, Dietrich Bonhoeffer felt himself the chosen servant of the word of Jesus Christ. By that time the prisons had become so overcrowded that the inmates could no longer be segregated. Bonhoeffer took advantage of this condition by arranging prayer services, consoling those who had lost all hope, and giving them fresh courage. A towering rock of faith, he became a shining example to his fellow prisoners.[31]

Bonhoeffer and several other men, including his brother-in-law, died because they tried to overthrow Hitler. They understood that obedience to authority must always be carefully evaluated in the light of God's love and justice. Prayer can lead to unexpected results. Bonhoeffer, according to James W. Woelfel, put it in perspective:

"Our being Christians today will be limited to two things: prayer and righteous action among men." "Secret" prayer by the individual Christian and within the church, and active, unassuming concern for the secular neighbor: that is all the church has left. But it is precisely the case that "all Christian thinking, speaking, and organizing must be born anew out of this prayer and action."[32]

The global community today still cries out for such depth of prayer. For Dietrich Bonhoeffer, the embodiment of God simply meant that God is in the center of one's life. One begins to mature when prayer comes from the center and trust in God's guidance grows, but God's guidance is often complex.

This point is particularly poignant with someone like Mother Teresa, who offered this prayer, "May the Lord keep you in his heart because it is the only place we can be together."[33] She has been criticized for her ministry of giving the poor a place to die with dignity. She didn't claim to be about changing systems. It seems cruel simply to help people die when poverty could be alleviated, but Mother Teresa was called to a particular ministry of the heart.

From her writings and all that has been written about her, a consistent theme weaves through the fabric of her life. She concentrated on deep prayer—prayer so deeply centered that rational thought could be transcended. Mother Teresa understood that through prayer one could be filled with the vastness of love required of the Christian. She concluded that every work of love brought one face to face with God, the meeting place for all people. It takes great strength to work with people debilitated by disease and hopelessness. Mother Teresa's formula for living that life of service is not complicated, but asks us to go deep.

Love to pray—feel the need to pray often during the day and take the trouble to pray. If you want to pray better, you must pray more. Prayer enlarges that heart until it is capable of containing God's gift of self.[34]

Pray—pray for grace, pray that you may understand how Jesus has loved you so that you may love others.... Perfect prayer does not consist in many words, but in the fervor and desire which raised the heart of Jesus.[35]

Mother Teresa clarified the prayer process: first, one must learn to listen; only in silence can one hear the beating of God's pulse. A clean heart is a prerequisite in order to hear, see, and listen to God. Prayer and contemplation are responses to the love of God.

When one's soul becomes one with God, there is energy to meet the Spirit of God in another—a child dying from hunger, a man looking for affirmation as disease eats his life, or a woman bewildered and lost through mental anguish. Only in that oneness with the Spirit of God can one do what would otherwise be impossible.

I was a guest in the home of a church member and his family when he shared his faith journey. In his mid-twenties, he had committed to travel with a mission group to India and work with the refugees from Bangladesh. He spoke of the time he was in a gathering with Mother Teresa.

The adjectives that flowed through his speech in reference to her presence were *humble, gracious, compassionate, servant-oriented*. In the gathering, she had remained at the back of the room operating the lights until someone needed her help. He later visited her and found the same characteristics shining forth.

It is the integrity of her prayer-directed faith that still awes those of us in the 21st century. She often spoke brief words of instruction to those who hungered for her level of righteousness and freely gave the map to anyone who wanted to follow her path. "Jesus does not say 'hold fast to the world' but 'love one another as I have loved you.' You cannot love as he did without prayer…. Through prayer you will believe and through belief you will love—through love you will serve."[36]

Those of us who diligently desire to follow the pattern of Jesus Christ learn through the life of Mother Teresa that prayer is the foundation for knowing the Spirit of God, and transformation is the consequence. In the sermon given in her honor after she received the Nobel

Prize for Peace, one can hear the challenge of being in a prayer-filled relationship with God:

> The love that we meet in Jesus is the love that overcomes all bound-aries and it is the same love that we find reflected in those who, throughout the history of the Church, have tried to follow in their Master's footsteps.

> If there is something that our divided world without peace needs then it is people who in the name of Christ will cross boundaries to lessen their neighbor's need, regardless of standing and reputation.[37]

Henri Nouwen is another spiritual leader whose work helped transform the lives of thousands. He made his life into a prayer-filled relationship with all who came into his presence. Henri devoted his adult life to experiencing the contentment that comes from living in the presence of God. He also viewed this life as a laboratory in which to experience transformation and to teach others about its product: joy. His laboratories included caring for the mentally and physically disabled, living in solitude in Nicaragua, and teaching in the contemporary classroom. Consistently, he discovered the value of a deep and enduring prayer life.

The "lab reports" concluded that the western way of life seemed to be problematic. We have become an impatient people. Doing is more important than praying. Whereas James said that faith without works is dead (James 2:14), Nouwen believed that action without prayer is futile. Prayer is the magnetic pull that moves one into intimacy with God. Nouwen's formula for developing a disciplined prayer life involved the following:

1. Do not run from the moment.
2. Listen carefully to people and observe events to discern the Spirit.
3. Keep mind and heart from being cluttered with what clamors for attention.
4. Intentionally create time to be alone with God and listen to the Spirit.

If one follows this formula, discernment and transformation are possible.

When transformation occurs through the Spirit, people grow closer to one another. One's responsibility for others grows. Nouwen expresses this concept:

> The Holy Spirit, the Spirit of peace, unity, and reconciliation, constantly reveals himself to us as the power through whom people from the most diverse social, political, economic, racial, and ethnic backgrounds are brought together as sisters and brothers of the same Christ and daughters and sons of the same Father.[38]

Thus, the ongoing prayer is to embrace others as a part of us. Prayer is the conduit for the healing power of God's Spirit. It is in and through us that relationships are restored; people receive new hope and courage. It is in and through us, as we pray, that God's Spirit touches another with a healing presence. Let the following Scriptures speak to your soul.[39]

> Matthew 21:22—"Everything you ask for in prayer you will receive."

> James 5:16—"The heartfelt prayer of a good man works very powerfully."

> Matthew 5:44—"I say this to you: love your enemies and pray for those who persecute you."

> Luke 23:34—"Father, forgive them; they do not know what they are doing."

Henri Nouwen notes that God created humans in order to be in relationship with them. Our task in prayer is always to move toward community and reconciliation. Relationships are the means of healing—whether physical, personal, or social. The prayer life Nouwen prescribed leads to social activism for God. Prayer without action grows into powerless pietism, and action without prayer lacks depth and can degenerate into questionable manipulation. As prayer leads us into deeper unity with Christ, it can give rise to concrete acts of service.

THE LORD'S PRAYER

Two Gospel texts give us the Lord's Prayer (NRSV):

Matthew 6:9-13	*Luke 11:2-4*
Our Father in heaven,	Father,
hallowed be your name.	hallowed be your name.
Your kingdom come.	Your kingdom come.
Your will be done,	
on earth as it is in heaven.	
Give us this day our daily	Give us each day our daily
bread.	bread.
And forgive us our debts,	And forgive us our sins,
as we also have forgiven	for we ourselves forgive
our debtors.	everyone indebted to us.
And do not bring us to the time	And do not bring us to the time
of trial,	of trial.
but rescue us from the evil one.	

A close look at the two texts helps us to see some critical differences. In Luke 11:1, the disciples ask Jesus how to pray. "He was praying in a certain place, and after he had finished, one of his disciples said to him, 'Lord, teach us to pray, as John taught his disciples.'"

Jesus then gives them the Lord's Prayer. However, in Matthew 6 there is already an ongoing assumption that prayer is part of the spiritual life of Jesus' followers.

> "Beware of practicing your piety before others in order to be seen by them; but then you have no reward from your Father in heaven." (Matthew 6:1)

"And whenever you pray, do not be like the hypocrites; for they love to stand and pray in the synagogues and at the street corners, so that they may be seen by others. Truly I tell you, they have received their reward. But whenever you pray, go into your room and shut the door and pray to your Father who is in secret; and your Father who sees in secret will reward you. When you are praying, do not heap up empty phrases as the Gentiles do; for they think that they will be heard because of their many words. Do not be like them, for your Father knows what you need before you ask him." (Matthew 6:5-8)

In Luke, Jesus set his face toward Jerusalem. In Matthew, the Lord's Prayer appears in the middle of the Sermon on the Mount and "uses stronger words and makes greater demands on those who pray it than does Luke's." Matthew's context is more social-gospel oriented, with Jesus rebelling against an unjust structure. The term used seven times in Matthew (3:15; 5:6, 10, 20; 6:1, 33; 21:32) is *dikaiosyne*—to do what is right; to do justice. Tertullian, in the third century, defined this prayer as "an epitome of the whole Gospel."[40]

One way to glean the meaning of the prayer is to look carefully at its context through reason, experience, and Scripture. Let's look closely at the content and structure of the Lord's Prayer. If Tertullian is right, we have much to gain. The Lord's Prayer consists of a) the address; b) two 'thou petitions' in parallel form (in Matthew, three); c) two 'we petitions' in parallel form; d) the concluding request; e) the added benediction.

The Address: *Our Father*

In the Old Testament, 14 passages refer to God as *father*. As Israel's father and from a position of power, this God elected, delivered, and saved people. Further development of God as father occurs in the messages from the prophets. Often accusatory, they claim that the people have not honored God by their choices in living (Deuteronomy 32:5). The depth of honor that a son should grant to his father is compared to that which the people should give God (Jeremiah 3:19).

A son honors his father, and a servant his master.
If then I am a father, where is my honor?
And if I am a master, where is my fear?
says the Lord of hosts. Malachi 1:6

In the New Testament, *father* changes in connotation. The common word for *father* was *abba,* an everyday word, a family word, like "dad," or "daddy," or "papa." With the exception of his cry from the cross (see Psalm 22:1), Jesus' conversations with God had the same tone that a child uses with his/her father—simple, intimate, secure. This manner of speaking contained his message, his claim to have been sent from the Father, and the kind of relationship with God he was teaching. In the Lord's Prayer, Jesus has his disciples repeat the word *abba* after him. In doing so, he gives his followers a place in God's family and empowers them to speak with the Heavenly Father in a trusting way. In order fully to achieve this relationship, Jesus instructs the disciples that unless they become children again, they "will not find entrance into the kingdom of God" (Matthew 18:3). Anyone can repeat the word *abba,* but not everyone can have child-like trust. A new relationship is in the birthing process; the doors to God's reign are opened to all; justice will be done.[41]

"You" Petitions: ... *hallowed be your name.*
                    Your Kingdom come.

These petitions are parallel in structure and content. They bring forth the revelation of God's kingdom. *Hallowed* is an action, not just a description. And God's presence is a kingdom, not just a personal experience. The Gospel Jesus preached was that God's kingdom has come near. Most of his parables were about God's kingdom. Implicitly, God's kingdom was always in contrast to the Roman kingdom—the empire occupying Israel during Jesus' time.

In Matthew, a third petition with similar meaning is added: "Your will be done, on earth as it is heaven." Together, these petitions cry out of the depths of distress. They were offered in a world of continuous conflict and evil. Within these petitions, the implication is that there must be an absolute trust that God will complete the salvation of God's people.

They are similar to the *Kaddish*—an ancient Aramaic prayer which completed a typical service in the synagogue. In childhood, Jesus would have learned this prayer:

Exalted and hallowed be his great name
    in the world which he created according to his will.
May he let his kingdom rule
    in your lifetime and in your days and in the lifetime
    of the whole house of Israel, speedily and soon.
And to this, say: amen.[42]

One of the most striking differences between the *Kaddish* and these two petitions is that in the *Kaddish* the praying person is requesting consummation sometime in the future. Life is being lived through a vision to be fulfilled. But the Lord's Prayer contains the understanding that God's saving work has already begun. The light of God's saving promise is revealing the pathway.

"We" Petitions: *Give us this day our daily bread.*

These petitions really are the heart of the Lord's Prayer. Asking for daily bread meant survival in a world where bread was not guaranteed. Beyond the request for earthly bread was a request for the symbolic bread of life. Since the time of Moses, bread and water were prominent symbols of life. Manna (bread) in the desert and water from a rock struck by Moses meant survival of God's people escaping the oppression of Egypt. This salvation brought all of God's material and spiritual gifts to the service of a free people. God is the bread of life.

At the Last Supper, where Jesus and the disciples remembered this escape from Egypt as they celebrated the Passover meal, the broken bread gained even more meaning. It became the Body of Christ given for many in death. Looking back, every meal that his disciples had with him could have easily appeared as just casual eating and drinking. Yet it was more. Every meal was a meal of salvation—a banquet exceeding all that earthly life could offer. Every meal was a meal in his presence. This bread mixed everyday life with a potent yeast: the power of God. The petition for the bread of life was a request for the hallowing of everyday life and the spiritual empowering of his followers.

One of the most intriguing aspects of the petition is the phrase "this day." This day for us presents a world where God seems to be so distant for so many. The hungering and thirsting, the evil acts of human beings, the obsession with greed and status all overpower the request for bread. It takes a powerful faith to reach now for the bread to come.[43]

<u>Forgiveness Petition</u>: *And forgive us our debts, as we also have forgiven our debtors*

In praying for forgiveness, the disciples recognized their human imperfection, their sin, the cracks in their relationships with God. They knew that forgiveness could not wait until tomorrow, for they did not know if life would be granted tomorrow. The present day was when the Messiah would offer the forgiveness needed for living in the presence of God.

The second half of this forgiveness petition emphasizes human activity. There is something lost in translation from Aramaic to English. In English, the use of *as* normally applies to a comparison being made. The Aramaic literally means: as we also herewith forgive our debtors. The one doing the praying is reminded of his/her own need to forgive.

One cannot ask for forgiveness if one cannot give it. In Mark 11:25, Jesus taught: "Whenever you stand praying, forgive, if you have anything against anyone; so that your Father also who is in heaven may forgive you your trespasses." Healing or repairing a broken relationship requires forgiveness (Matthew 5:23). We must willingly offer forgiveness in one hand as the other hand reaches out to receive God's forgiveness.

<u>Final request</u>: *And do not bring us to trial, but rescue us from the evil one.*

These words are a petition for preservation. It is the only petition in the negative and has been regarded as harsh and abrupt. The modern version of this petition reads: "do not lead us into temptation but deliver us from evil." Because the verb *lead* is used, the request echoes an ancient Jewish evening prayer that would have been familiar to Jesus.

> Lead my foot not into the power of sin
> And bring me not into the power of iniquity,
> And not into the power of temptation
> And not into the power of anything shameful.[44]

There is an ancient extra-canonical saying of Jesus prior to the prayer in Gethsemane:

> No man can obtain the kingdom of heaven
> That hath not passed through temptation.[45]

The one who prays will not be spared temptation, but God will help one to live through it and overcome. Temptation in this context does not mean little temptations or testings of everyday life. It refers to the powerful testings that lurk in every corner and put faith at risk.

<u>Blessing</u>: *For thine is the kingdom and the power and the glory forever. Amen.*

This Doxology cannot be found in either of the Gospel texts. It was first found in the *Didache*. It apparently seemed erroneous that the Lord's Prayer had no closing words of praise to God. In Palestinian religious gatherings, no prayer would have ended on a thought of temptation. In the Jewish tradition, prayers ended with a "seal"—a freely formed doxology. When the Lord's Prayer began to be prayed in services, it was felt necessary to add a doxology.[46]

Reflection

The opening of the prayer calls us into relationship with God that remains our task to perfect. It is just as critical now, as it was in Matthew's culture, to reflect with integrity of heart, mind, and action the values which emerge from this prayer.[47]

LEARNING FROM
PRAYER PATTERNS

As I live my prayer life and converse with others about theirs, I am reminded continually of an old expression: "Different strokes for different folks." The art of prayer could never be limited to one pattern, for art is an expression of creativity and continual change. Whether one is making art to honor the almighty creative Spirit, designing a worship center, or playing a melody, there is always the reality of a Presence that blesses these activities.

I spend most of my time in ministry being a detective—discerning clues that will bring wholeness to another's life. Detecting, too, is a description of prayer, as we discern the presence of God wherever we happen to be at any moment. Many teachers and students have sought to discern and perfect methods of praying. The foci and styles of praying are as diverse as all creation.

Patterns of Prayer and Action

Those who have heard the call to a life of prayer and action enlist the power of God through prayer to bring forth social change. Martin Luther King, Jr.'s, prayer life compelled him to confront systems contrary to the New Testament. As he lived with those afflicted by racial bigotry, he depended upon the presence of God in his life to direct his actions.

Early in his ministry, the Montgomery, Alabama, bus boycott took place. Dr. King joined with other clergy and civic leaders to create a new understanding of dignity for all persons. In the struggle for justice, violent opposition swirled.

One night, in the midst of one of the most heated times of the struggle, Dr. King received an anonymous, life-threatening phone call. In his book, *Strength to Love*, he wrote:

> I got out of bed and began to walk the floor. Finally, I went to the kitchen and heated a pot of coffee. I was ready to give up. I tried to think of a way to move out of the picture without appearing to be a coward. In this state of exhaustion when my courage had almost gone, I determined to take my problem to God. My head in my hands, I bowed over the kitchen table and prayed aloud. The words I spoke to God that midnight are still vivid in my memory. "I am here taking a stand for what I believe is right. But now I am afraid. The people are looking to me for leadership, and if I stand before them without strength and courage, they too will falter. I am at the end of my powers. I have nothing left. I've come to the point where I can't face it alone."
>
> At that moment I experienced the presence of the Divine as I had never before experienced him. It seemed as though I could hear the quiet assurance of an inner voice, saying, "Stand up for righteousness, stand up for truth. God will be at your side forever." Almost at once my fears began to pass from me. My uncertainty disappeared. I was ready to face anything. The outer situation remained the same, but God had given me an inner calm.
>
> Three nights later, our home was bombed. Strangely enough, I accepted the word of the bombing calmly. My experience with God had given me a new strength and trust. I knew now that God is able to give us the interior resources to face the storms and problems of life.[48]

This passage reveals the way to gain strength through prayer. As an apostle of nonviolence, Martin Luther King, Jr., knew that knowledge of God would be able to sustain him through the trials. He depended upon the example of followers from long ago. A heart filled with the Spirit of God enables strength to flow through the veins and arteries. A creative substance begins flowing, changing life and initiating action.

Movement meant change, change meant friction, and friction meant controversy. But King knew that genuine prayer requires an opening of the heart and mind for God's will to be done. His life is similar to that of Moses, Jesus, Paul, Teresa of Avila, John Wesley, Bonhoeffer, and others who saw injustices being inflicted upon God's people. Divine strength can make it possible to stand against oppression.

Prayer can make a difference only if, after we get up from our knees, we don't sit down to rest. As King said, "The idea that man expects God to do everything, leads inevitably to a callous misuse of prayer. For if God does everything, man then asks him for anything, and God becomes little more than a 'cosmic bellhop' who is summoned for every trivial need."

Jesus spoke of sending his followers into an alien and antagonistic world in John 17 during the high priestly prayer. The trials are still present, and the divine strength is still flowing through those who serve as prayer activists for all of God's people.

Patterns of Singing Our Prayers

Songs of freedom have accompanied many along the way of the cross. For those on a pilgrimage to know God, freedom flows.

The black gospel songs are an important source of emotional support and spiritual power for persons committed to social change. Such persons bring to their worship a concern rooted in their own experience of hardship, their biblical insights, their personal thought and prayer, and understanding gained from discussion with others. Though the songs may not focus directly on the changes sought, they may reinforce convictions reached on other grounds, strengthen community awareness, and deepen the consciousness of the worshipers that God is with them in their struggle. Songs like "Precious Lord" strengthened the resolve of Martin Luther King, Jr., even though Dorsey's lyric says not a word about jobs, education, housing, or desegregation.... Christians who seek fullness of life for all God's children can find spiritual power through opening their hearts in worship to the God who wants all to be free.[49]

United Methodist Women members have long been committed to singing about freedom in Christ. In my experience, these women have been deeply passionate and generous in their love for God. Their pledges to their local UMW units are held in prayer; with the dawning of the day and the setting of the sun, they offer prayer; the service for the Call to Prayer and Self-Denial is a priority; the prayers offered for the care and calling of missionaries are not printed for someone else to read; their giving is incredible when the call comes to care for another; they meet the challenge to study God's global community and to care for God's creation. They sing with joy, "What a friend we have in Jesus, all our sins and griefs to bear! What a privilege to carry everything to God in prayer!"[50] They nurture their relationship with God by praying: "Have thine own way, Lord! Have thine own way! Thou art the potter; I am the clay. Mold me and make me after thy will, while I am waiting, yielded and still."[51]

The faithful give themselves unconditionally as they sing the songs of Mary, Ruth, Elizabeth, Hannah, Martha, Esther, Rahab, Jochebed, Hagar, and Rachel. What will the songs of prayer be for the days ahead? The rhythms may be altered, but the words will still lift the heart to God.

Psalms

The sung prayer of salvation and commitment is an ancient one. The psalmists are the greatest composers of prayer. Whether we read or study them, the Psalms are a prayer-filled source of direction. The psalmists include many emotions and moods and speak of social injustices, historical facts, human frailties, images of pure beauty, and the coldness of evil.

Because of the rhythmic language, many verses have a memorable flow and were originally sung. Although we don't have the ancient melodies, the patterns encourage repetition and quick memorization. The Psalms are an excellent source for *lectio divina,* divine reading. One chooses a Psalm or part of a Psalm as a guide in prayer. The necessary ingredients of *lectio divina* are:

1. to read the word—read the passage slowly, and jot down those words that strike a chord within you.
2. to ponder the word—stay with the part that most attracts you and converse with God about what makes this section meaningful.
3. to pray the word—become aware of what God is saying to you; visualize an image or insight, or desire to do something.
4. to rest in the word—be silent with God's presence in and around you; put your feelings into writing.
5. to live the word—true prayer ultimately results in action, but listening comes first; what is the word asking of you?

The discipline required is listening. If one learns to listen, God can be honest with the listener. In listening prayer, one must move away from the idea of doing something, quiet the incessant talking in the mind, and then make space in order to hear God. "Be still and know that I am God!" (Psalm 46:10).

The hymnbook of ancient Israel was the Psalms. One found there the appropriate expressions to give praise to God. Thanksgiving is gratitude for God's gifts, and praise is gratitude for God's being who God is. The lives of prayer-givers past substantiate for us that the more grateful one is for what has been given, the more openness there is to receive God's gifts. The sweetness of prayer is a grateful heart. Hymn writers of recent times continue to draw upon the Psalms. A favorite chorus lifts the power of Psalm 103:1-2: "Bless the Lord, O my soul, and all that is within me, bless his holy name. Bless the Lord, O my soul, and do not forget all his benefits."

Cultural Prayer Patterns

Every culture makes a contribution to prayer patterns. Whether it is the passionate early morning petitions of Koreans or the on-your-knees prayers in Africa, culture and context shape our prayer patterns. Many Native Americans recognize the interconnectedness of all creation and the responsibility of human beings to protect the water, air, soil, etc.

The emphasis is upon long-term welfare rather than short-term expediency or comfort. Issues and actions that affect all life, not just human life, are considered.

Two stories about prayer from Native American traditions illustrate these elements. Here, the foundation for spirituality is thankfulness to the Creator.

The Seneca Iroquois' Sacrifice Flower prayer is explained by Sister Jose Hobday of the Order of St. Francis. Her mother taught her to say the prayer when her heart was heavy and she wanted a fresh breath of air. Her mother would have her go or accompany her outside to find a sacrifice flower. The flower was supposed to be unique and hold special significance. Because it was considered precious, they would carefully take it inside and tell it their burden or concern. As life left the flower, it would absorb the burden and carry it to God. The flower would be placed in a prominent setting where the slow sacrifice, the losing of life, could be visible. It did not matter how long it took for life to drain completely from the flower, for in those hours and days, the burden was being carried to God.

When death finally overcame the flower, there would be a burial for the flower, in which one would say goodbye to it and thank it for giving its life for another's burden. This was a simple and poignant way to experience the uplifting power of prayer and to teach the significance of becoming sacrificial flowers for others, like Jesus.[52]

The second illustration of prayer, from the Cherokee tradition, is explained by Steve Dawson Blaze Blazina, Methodist pastor. He tells of his experience working with youth in a camp setting. Benny, a Cherokee, offers to teach the participants about prayer.

"*Where is God?* Some Cherokees believe that God is a passenger, a stowaway in your breath. God bears witness to everything we say. Let us pray." He turned to the *East* with an eagle feather held high in the air and asked us stand and follow him as he prayed to God in the sacred directions of creation. He began, "Merciful Creator, thank you for the sun which purifies. It brings light into the world, enlightenment into the darkness, and understanding to the ignorant. Help us to be bearers of your light." Turning to the **South**, he said, "Creator of life, thank you for times of growth. Thank you for nurturing us, helping us to grow, for blessing us and enabling us to be a blessing to others." Turning to the **West**, he said, "Father of our ancestors, thank you for the stories of your faithfulness to your people. Grant us the ears to listen to you and the wisdom to live accordingly." Turning to the **North**, he said, "Great Creator, thank you for the snow that winter brings. It purifies the earth and allows your creation to become renewed. You freeze life in mid-breath, holding it until you say it may live again so that we will remember always the mystery and our own humility. Thank you for the seasons of winter in our lives. It is the facing of such trials that allows you to renew our lives. Grant us the strength to endure them." Turning *toward the earth*, he said, "Creator, we give you thanks for providing for our every need, for calling us out of the earth and seeking a relationship with each of us, and for granting us the opportunity to be in sacred relationship with you and all of your creation." Turning *inward*, he said, "We pray in all of these directions, remembering your faithfulness, and with all of who we are, *(then raising his hands **toward** heaven)* we offer our prayers and ourselves to you this day." [53]

As one reflects upon these two illustrations, it becomes quite obvious how life is as "broad as beach and meadow, wide as the wind" (from the hymn "Your Love, O God," *United Methodist Hymnal*, #120). All of creation belongs to God, and should be embraced and respected as a treasure. Life is incredibly connected.

Black Elk's view paints the picture with the most brilliant colors:

We regard all created beings as sacred and important, for everything has influence, which can be given to us, through which we may gain a little more understanding if we are attentive. We should understand well that all things are the works of the Great Spirit. We should know that He is with all things; the trees, the grasses, the rivers, the mountains and all the four-legged animals, and the winged creatures; and even more important, we should understand that He is also above all these things and people.

Nature provides an ongoing adventure for the one who has prayer at the center of the heart. In Matthew 6:28b ("Consider the lilies....") and in many parables (cf. the sower, Matthew 13:24-30), Jesus taught that there is much to glean from all of creation.

Patterns of Prayer in Nature

This understanding of God's presence is amazingly similar to that of St. Francis of Assisi. "He loves to see in all around him the pulsations of one life, which sleeps in the stones, dreams in the plants, and wakens in man."[54] He was inspired by the interdependent design of God's creation. The plant depended upon the sun and replenished the air. So strong was his conviction that all living things were children of God that he would preach even to his little sisters, the birds.

Prayer is having a relationship with God and all of God's creation. Neither the Native Americans of old nor St. Francis would have used terms like ozone, nuclear waste, dirty bombs, water pollution, wildlife preservation, biological warfare, carcinogens, or collateral damage. Are we modeling a life of prayer by embracing all of God's creation for the future? Reflect on the beloved prayer/song of St. Francis of Assisi, "Make Me a Channel of Your Peace," at the end of this chapter.

Finding Your Prayer Patterns

There are many helpful patterns of praying. The pattern of praying that is best for one person is not necessarily best for another. The important thing is to be diligent in finding yours. In Matthew 6:5-6, Jesus instructs the listeners how to pray. "Do not pray like the hypocrites... but go to your room and shut the door and pray...." Praying with other Christians was very important in the early Christian community. However, Jesus had personally discovered through his struggles with temptation that strength came when one prayed alone with God. Most of us today suffer from the inability to make time for the Creator. Once we set a pattern for conversing with God, the process becomes as familiar as putting on the oldest but most comfortable clothes.

We can pray in a variety of ways: journaling, using prayers others have authored, looking at something in nature, meditating silently, using guided prayer tapes, listening to music, praying during a walk or run, or creating a worship center with symbols that are visually empowering.

A pattern often included in time alone with God is intercessory prayer. Intercession happens when we commend someone else to God. Offering someone to be washed in the grace of God is ministry in its purest form. An excellent reference from Scripture is Mark 2:1-12, in which the townspeople lower the paralytic through the roof of the house in Capernaum so that Jesus could heal him.

As baptized members of a community of faith, we are called to pray for those in need. As our hearts begin to develop peripheral vision, our prayers change to "God, give through me.... Make me a channel of your peace."

As channels for God's activity, we become change agents for those in need, to reach, to save, to bless people.

What is the best way to intercede? Some believe the less specific the better; others believe in praying only what they think is best for the other person. Other people want to know exactly what to pray for and then to pray for specific results. In the end, intercession is inviting God to work in a person or situation in God's way, no one else's way. What is said and how it is said matters little.

Simple breath prayers, such as "Jesus healer, make her whole," are to the point. Perhaps just mentally picturing the person or concern would be effective. What matters most is bringing the person or situation to Jesus for healing, just as the paralyzed man's friends brought him to Jesus. To hold another in prayer is to feel the weight of the concern.

In prayer, one asks God to share the weight. Some people find it easy to visualize Jesus with the person in need; others do not. According to Scripture, God knows, cares, and loves. Thus, we have a prayer such as, "Lord Jesus / have mercy on [name]; Lord Jesus / have mercy on them."

What about the times, and they do occur, when one just cannot pray? Despair and the sense of being forsaken by God can become overwhelming. Romans 8:26 can give us comfort for those times: "[The] Spirit helps us in our weakness; for we do not know how to pray as we ought, but the Spirit himself intercedes for us with sighs too deep for words." There will be times when others will have to intercede on our behalf. We hesitate to ask someone to pray for our needs because our culture teaches us to take care of ourselves. Great strength comes when another person reaches out to take our hand in prayer. The channel of grace deepens and widens, and the waters of hope and healing wash over the soul.

One of the greatest gifts I have received from God was having a prayer mentor. The lay leader in a local appointment proposed such a relationship. She believed that prayer is the strength that would hold pastor and laity together. Our prayer time was devoted more to intercession than to any other kind of praying. Sometimes it was as smooth as everyday conversation. But there was always the recognition of the other's deep need or desire. Over the years, it became a significant well from which I could fill my cup. We always concluded with Philippians 1:9-10: "And this is my prayer, that your love may overflow more and more with true knowledge and full insight to help you determine what is best, so that in the day of Christ you may be pure and blameless."

Patterns of Church

The liturgy and ritual of worship services provide the opportunity for the gathered church, the community of believers baptized in the faith, to pray together regardless of personal differences. "They devoted themselves to the apostles' teaching and fellowship, to the breaking of bread and the prayers." (Acts 2:42) Corporate praying establishes a supportive community through the connecting Spirit. Praying the liturgy keeps one from being self-absorbed. Individual feelings and needs are not central. Prayer among the community of believers means there is no one person in charge. For all present, the focus is to move from an individual to a global perspective, from one's own want list to the concerns of others.

No one stands alone. Let us claim our part in the cooperative adventure to pray for the concerns and commitments, the hopes and visions, the joys and struggles of all of God's children.

Make Me a Channel of Your Peace
by St. Francis of Assissi

Lord, make me a channel of your peace;
where there is hatred, let me bring your love;
where there is injury, your pardon;
where there is doubt, true faith in you;
where there is despair in life, let me bring hope;
where there is darkness, only light;
and where there is sadness, ever joy.

O Master, grant that I may never seek
so much to be consoled, as to console;
to be understood, as to understand;
to be loved, as to love with all my soul!
For it is in pardoning that we are pardoned,
in giving of ourselves that we receive,
and in dying that we are born to eternal life.

Amen.

V

PRAYING INTO THE TOMORROWS

William James, the American philosopher, said, "Many reasons have been given why we should not pray, while others are given why we should. But in all this very little is said of the reason why we do pray. The reason why we pray is simply that we cannot help praying." The desire to pray is with us as we enter life. Some refer to it as instinct; others contend that it is a learned process. I believe that the desire is innate, but certain aspects of praying are learned.

Once we learn the precepts of prayer, perfecting our practice of prayer shapes our spiritual life, and our relationship with God stands on a firmer foundation. We can then engage in powerful ministry in conjunction with the Spirit of God.

Martin Luther best expressed the first principle for a life centered in prayer: "Don't lie to God." Typically, one couches prayer in language that contains melodious strands of piety, but we may be missing honesty. In praying—spoken or silent—the heart longs to be fully revealed. This is the first requirement of honesty. The prayer of the revealed heart is an open invitation. "God, fill my heart with your Spirit." God knows the secrets of the heart and knows when you ask for blessings or intervention but do not truly expect to receive. A relationship with God requires honesty.

The second requirement is that prayer must be unambiguous. It is too easy when misery invades to ask for forgiveness; the cause of the misery should be named.

Honest reflection makes praying hard spiritual work. Self-examination is difficult, exhausting, and sometimes embarrassing. We live much of our lives trying to escape such moments of intense work. Thus, Wesley's inner discipline is necessary in developing an intimate relationship with God and integrating the need to pray with honest self-examination. Confession requires honesty.

Along with personal honesty, effective prayer engages relationships and responsibility. God listens not just to one person praying but to everyone. Though "one" may seem to be the only number that matters in praying, collectively the "ones" comprise an infinite quantity. Literally, one affects another. Therefore, God cannot indulge our selfish desires. As atoms make up an object, so all persons form the family of God. Errant behavior within a family is never conducive for the betterment of all. So it is with individual prayer requests.

A dear friend of mine who has earnestly nurtured a spiritual life reminds me periodically of the importance of viewing the big picture. The big picture is what the eyes of God behold. Though one may pray for something of considerable value today, the request may not ultimately lead to lasting goodness. God sees time's vista and may regard a moment's prayer request as short-sighted. A look back on our past prayer requests can show what different paths life would have taken if they had been granted.

The lack of an answer to prayer often leaves one in a horrible state of doubt—even questioning the presence of God. Ultimately, unanswered prayer does not exist. Sometimes in the anxiety of the moment we forget that there are more answers than "yes" and "no." One of them is "wait," as in wait and see the total design that God in time will give.

God gives abilities and expects us to use them to accomplish things. Individuals need to assume the responsibility of acting in conjunction with God. In the years I taught English, sad students on the day of final exams sometimes said they hoped God was with them. Without a miracle, they had no hope of passing the exams. God had given them the ability to learn, but they had chosen not to use it.

Prayer requires heart and mind working together. This is the formula: Human effort plus the grace of God equals the discovery of God's answer. In Ezekiel 2:1, God says: "Son of man, stand on thy feet and I will speak to thee." Today, God tells us to move from the comfort of the recliner and be spiritually, mentally, and physically engaged in a life of prayer. In the connection, answers will come.

One cannot ignore the reality of natural laws. Gravity is a natural law. No amount of prayer can prevent my falling to the ground after I have tripped. The suspension of gravity would create chaos for all creation!

Sometimes prayer requests during a worship service seem to reveal a reluctance to accept the reality of natural laws. Periodically, there are requests for rain for the farmer's crops and sunny days for family outdoor activities. So often, prayer contains a desire to avoid a particular situation. There is no need to seek avoidance. Prayer exudes power. Natural laws cannot be altered by prayer, but these prayers are a way of turning over our worries to God. God gives strength to endure any situation. The prayer I eventually offer is for acceptance and gratitude for whatever God gives.

Prayer brings power and endurance to stay the course and overcome. The Scriptures are sprinkled with such illustrations. A powerful scene takes place in the Garden of Gethsemane. Jesus prayed that if it were God's will, he would prefer to be released from the cross. God did not grant the request; however, God did grant Jesus the sustaining power to meet and endure the cross.

"Seek first the kingdom of God and its righteousness, and then all other things will be given to you." (Matthew 6:33) This should be the direction of everyone's prayer life. As long as one's own desires and requests take preeminence, the kingdom remains distant. Kierkegaard writes, "Prayer does not change God. It changes the one who prays." Listening to the still small voice and claiming the value of inner quiet will bring about change.

In conclusion, prayer keeps us moving into the tomorrows. Prayer is the optic nerve of the soul, and heart-vision is critical for discerning the paths toward the kingdom. Let me close with the following principal points:

- Prayer challenges us.
- Prayer turns us around and makes us new.
- Prayer breaks down barriers of fear.
- Through prayer we enter a spiritual realm.
- A life of prayer is more demanding than any other calling.
- In prayer we die with Christ so as to live with him.

- In prayer we surrender everything.
- In prayer we divest ourselves of all false possessions.
- Prayer empowers us to act.
- Prayer patterns are shaped by culture and context.
- Prayer frees us to belong to God and God alone.
- In prayer we die to all that we consider to be our own.
- Through prayer we rise to a spiritual life.
- Through prayer we get direction for taking action.
- Prayer can make us joyful even when times are depressing.
- Prayer can give us peace when the threat of war is all around.
- Prayer can give us hope even when we face despair.

I begin each sermon with a familiar prayer: "Let the words of my mouth and the meditation of my heart, be acceptable in thy sight, O Lord, my strength, and my redeemer." (Psalm 19:14) It has also become my prayer for every day that God grants me. Prayer is the speech of solitude, the voice within the mind. It enables me to be aware of God's presence. The Great Comforter relieves my anxiety, and I feel safe. Only then am I fully receptive to hear and appropriate the Word that comes in any situation. I base all aspects of my daily life on prayer. In prayer I move into the tomorrows and invite you to continue living a life centered in prayer. So let it be. Amen!

Endnotes

1. *The United Methodist Hymnal* (Nashville: Abingdon Press, 1989), p. 492.

2. Brant D. Baker, *Teaching P.R.A.Y.E.R.: Guidance for Pastors and Church Leaders* (Nashville: Abingdon Press, 2001), p. 60.

3. Harvey Potthoff, *The Inner Life* (Nashville: Graded Press, 1969), p. 146.

4. Ibid, p. 149.

5. Joachim Jeremias, *The Prayers of Jesus* (Naperville, IL: Allenson, Inc., 1967), pp. 67-68.

6. Ibid., pp. 69-70.

7. Ibid., pp. 72-74.

8. Ibid., pp. 75-78.

9. "Old Creeds in a New World," from *This I Believe: II*, edited by Taymond Seuing (New York: Simon and Schuster, Help, Inc., 1954), p. 67.

10. Douglas V. Steere, *Dimensions of Prayer* (Nashville: The Upper Room General Board of Discipleship, 1997), p. 23.

11. Umphrey Lee, *John Wesley and Modern Religion* (Nashville: Cokesbury, 1936), pp. 107-108.

12. Francis L. Gross, Jr., *The Making of a Mystic* (State University of New York Press, 1993), p. 187.

13. Ibid., pp. 187-188.

14. Ibid., p. 203.

15. Ibid., pp. 26-27.

16. Ibid., pp. 209-210.

17. Steven Fanning, *Mystics of the Christian Tradition* (New York: Routledge, 2001), p. 82.

18. Ibid., p. 83.

19. *Hildegard of Bingen: Cosmic Christ, Religion of Experience, God the Mother, Part I*, http://www.sol.com.au/kor/5_02.htm

20. Ibid.

21. "Alive Now," from *The Upper Room*, July/August 1988, p. 35.

22. John Wesley, "A Plain Account of Christian Perfection," http://gbgm-umc.org/UMhistory/Wesley/plainaccount.stm

23. Fanning, p. 185.

24. Umphrey Lee, *John Wesley and Modern Religion* (Nashville: Cokesbury, 1936), pp. 107-108.

25. Ibid., p. 108.

26. David A. DeSilva, *Praying with John Wesley* (Nashville: Discipleship Resources, 2001), p. 5.

27. *John Wesley's Theology: A Collection from His Works*, edited by Robert W. Burtner and Robert E. Chiles (Nashville: Abingdon Press, 1982), pp. 229-230.

28. Ibid., p. 231

29. James W. Woelfel, *Bonhoeffer's Theology: Classical and Revolutionary* (Nashville: Abingdon Press, 1970), pp. 19-23.

30. Ibid., p. 202.

31. Ibid., pp. 203-204.

32. Ibid., p. 180.

33. Kathryn Spink, *The Miracle of Love* (New York: Harper and Row, 1981), p. 158.

34. Ibid., p. 66.

35. Kathryn Spink, *Life in the Spirit: Mother Teresa of Calcutta: Reflections, Meditations, Prayers* (HarperSanFrancisco, 1983), pp. 17-18.

36. Kathryn Spink, *The Miracle of Love* (San Francisco: Harper and Row 1981), pp. 31-33.

37. Kathryn Spink, *Life in the Spirit*, p. 86.

38. McNeill, Morrison, and Nouwen, *Compassion* (New York: Doubleday and Co., Inc., 1982), p. 108.

39. Ibid., pp. 110-111.

40. Michael Crosby, *The Prayer that Jesus Taught Us* (Maryknoll, New York: Orbis Books, 2001), p. 4.

41. Joachim Jeremias, *The Prayers of Jesus*, pp. 96-97.

42. Ibid., p. 98.

43. Ibid., pp. 100-101.

44. Ibid., p. 104.

45. Tertullian De baptismo, in Joachim Jeremias, *Unknown Sayings of Jesus* (London: SPCK 1964), pp. 73-75.

46. Joachim Jeremias, *The Prayers of Jesus,* pp. 20-22.

47. Michael Crosby, *The Prayer that Jesus Taught Us*, pp. 20-22.

48. Martin Luther King, Jr., *Strength to Love* (New York: Harper & Row, 1963), p. 107.

49. S. Paul Schilling, *The Faith We Sing* (Philadelphia, Pennsylvania: Westminster Press, 1983), pp. 194-195.

50. "What a Friend We Have in Jesus," *The United Methodist Hymnal*, (Nashville: Abingdon Press, 1989), p. 526.

51. "Have Thine Own Way, Lord," *The United Methodist Hymnal*, (Nashville: Abingdon Press, 1989), p. 382.

52. Jose Hobday. The sacrifice flower story is in public domain. For more of Sister Hobday's narratives, see: *Stories of Awe and Abundance* (New York: Continuum International Publishing Group, 1999).

53. Steve Dawson Blaze Blazina, "Teach Us to Pray," in *Gifts from the Heart*, compiled by Alyne JoAnn Catolster (Nashville: General Board of Discipleship, 2000), pp. 24-25. http://www.gbod.org.smallgroup/gifts/teach_pray.html

54. W. R. Inge, *Christian Mysticism* (Ohio: The World Publishing Company, 1964), pp. 301-302.

STUDY GUIDE BY MAXINE WEST

INTRODUCTION

This study guide is designed for use in local/district units of United Methodist Women and other study groups in local churches with the 2003-2004 spiritual growth study *Concerning Prayer*. This guide provides resources, suggestions, activities, and opportunities for study leaders and study groups to:

- deepen their knowledge and understanding of the dimensions and power of prayer
- examine their prayer lives in relation to the disciplined prayer lives of Jesus and other biblical and contemporary spiritual icons
- explore methods and aids for developing a more in-depth prayer life
- practice what they've learned within a supportive faith community of Christian women and men.

This guide includes plans for four two-hour sessions. The first three sessions relate to the first four chapters of the study book. Session four deals specifically with chapter five. Each session includes the purpose, suggested worship resources, small group discussion questions, experiential learning activities, and individual and group assignments.

It is our hope and prayer that this study will be a means of leading its users to a new depth of spiritual awareness as they engage in individual and group activities and use the many resources provided in the study book and guide.

To the Leader

As a study leader, your role is to help create a climate where learning can occur. One way to create such a climate is to establish expectations for participants. You will want to ensure that all participants will be respected, listened to, and supported in their efforts to learn. You will set the tone for each session by being yourself, showing interest in participants, welcoming diverse opinions, and providing positive responses and encouragement.

You are not expected to be the expert on the subject of prayer and should not feel that you have all the answers. As participants engage in the study, they will bring their own experiences to the learning process. Keep in mind that adults learn in a variety of ways. Your role is to use different teaching methods and processes as you provide opportunities for class members to use the resources and activities prepared for the study.

Ground Rules and Guidelines for the Study

The following ground rules and guidelines are adapted from "Guidelines for Class Participation" prepared by Nancy A. Carter in *Jesus in the Gospel of Matthew: "Who Do You Say That I Am?"*

Guidelines for Class Participation

Everyone is invited to participate; everyone also has the choice not to join in any activity. A study group should be spiritually, emotionally, and physically safe and a place for exciting learning. Below are some guidelines for doing this:

1. Listen with respect. Allow each person room to express opinions. There is no one right answer on which everyone must agree. Be open to different viewpoints and then make your own decisions. It is all right to disagree. We often learn more when we hear different opinions.

2. Speak long enough to convey your point but not so long that others do not have enough time to share. Speak the truth, as you best know it, with love. Come to each session with a positive attitude.

3. We are all members of God's holy family. It is not all right to attack a person's humanity or religious commitment because she or he has a different viewpoint. This is abuse.

4. Loving confrontation is appropriate. Ask the person to clarify a statement first. Paraphrase the statement, saying, "I heard you say...is that right?" Then share your perspective with the person. Sometimes it helps to use "feeling statements," such as "When you said [or did]..., I felt [uncomfortable, sad, angry] because (if there is a *because*)...."

5. Discussion is usually best at a personal and/or informational level. Try to make "I" statements about your own experience rather than

responding to others with phrases such as "You should do...." or "You should believe...."

6. Keep the personal sharing of others confidential. "Confidential" means the information does not leave the room and is not to be discussed with anyone not present in the room at the time the information was shared. Unless someone says it is okay to share something personal outside the room, assume it is confidential.

7. Some groups express friendship through touching and hugging. Some people are not comfortable with being touched. Before hugging or touching a person, be sure to ask, "Would you like a hug?" Do this verbally or by responding to the other person's body language. A "no" is not a personal rejection of you. The person is simply doing what is best for herself/himself.

Study Leader's Preparation

The study leader is responsible for setting the stage for a meaningful learning experience for participants. Early preparation on the part of the study leader can enhance the learning process. The following steps should be included in the study leader's preparation:

1. Read the study book carefully and become familiar with other basic resources related to the study.

2. Review suggested activities and discussion questions printed in the study guide, and make a list of items needed for each class activity.

3. Review the bibliography at the end of the study book and purchase or borrow as many books as you are able to find. Extensive reading on the topic of prayer will increase your knowledge of the subject and help you to be a better prepared leader.

4. Develop an outline for each class session that contains detailed time allocations for each component. Adjustments can be made as needed to allow for flexibility. Allow ample time during each session for questions and group discussions.

5. Make a list of any materials or items you might need to prepare ahead of time for the sessions.

6. Consider materials needed for creating a worship center that will serve as a focus for worship during each session.

Classroom Setting

The study leader is responsible for creating a climate that helps build community and enhances learning.

1. Where possible, arrange for the study group to meet in a room with moveable chairs or desks. To encourage study group participation and interaction, arrange chairs or desks in semicircles or concentric circles. Allow for open space for ease of movement and activities.

2. Create a worship center to serve as the focus for times of worship and meditation. You may want to change the worship center for each session or invite study group participants to contribute materials for the worship center at the beginning of each session.

3. Enhance the appearance of the classroom by creating displays consisting of posters, art work, quotes, and pictures of the spiritual icons related to the study. Where permissible, place displays on the walls with masking tape.

4. Use tables to display books and other resources for use in the class. Depending on the size of the study group, one or more tables will be needed for individual and group activities.

5. The classroom should be equipped with newsprint, easel, and magic markers. Chalkboards with chalk will be adequate if newsprint is not available. Other supplies that will be useful to have in the classroom include construction paper, large poster paper, 3" x 5" index cards, yarn (several color skeins or balls), scissors, colored markers, masking tape, adhesive tape or glue, a *2004 Prayer Calendar*, old copies of magazines, including old issues of *Response* and *New World Outlook*.

6. You will need a TV hooked up to a VCR, a CD/cassette player, and recorded music. Choose music that helps create a quiet, meditative environment, such as Celtic or sacred instrumental music.

Pre-assignment for Study-Group Participants

As a study-group leader, you will want to send a mailing to study-group participants prior to the first session. Secure the mailing list of class participants from the registrar or person responsible for registration. Introduce yourself as the study leader and welcome participants to the study. Be enthusiastic and let them know that they are about to take another important step on their spiritual journey toward wholeness. Encourage them to purchase the study book and, if time permits, read the introduction and chapter one before coming to the first class session.

Creating a Prayer Book

Either provide notebooks or ask in the letter to the participants that they each bring a notebook for collecting prayers, images, and reflections to form a personal prayer book. Ask participants to begin creating their prayer books before coming to the first session. They will need a note-book and pictures of peaceful landscapes, happy children, families, animals, etc. They can cut out pictures from magazines or use personal photos. When they come across a wonderful quotation, hymn, or Psalm about prayer, have them copy it into the book using multicolored pens opposite a picture. Participants will continue to create their prayer books during class time.

SESSION I

PRAYER

Purpose

- To introduce the focus and key concepts of the study as presented in the introduction and chapter one of the study book
- To examine Jesus' prayer life and the place of prayer as a spiritual discipline
- To engage study group members in a discussion of the meaning of prayer and the place of prayer in their own lives

Leader's Preparation for the Session

1. Bring the following materials for group activities: newsprint, colored markers, masking tape, felt pens, sheets of 5" x 8" card stock (enough for all participants), poster paper, 3" x 5" index cards, yarn, and the *2004 Prayer Calendar.*

2. Have copies of *The United Methodist Hymnal* available for participants.

3. Focus the study on the five definitions of prayer. Using the definitions of prayer chart in the study guide, make a poster for display in the classroom.

4. Create a large prayer mobile for display in the room. The mobile should consist of all definitions of prayer found in the introduction and chapter one of the study book. Instructions for creating a prayer mobile are on page 60 of the study guide.

5. As participants enter the room, welcome them and introduce yourself. Give them each a 5" x 8" piece of card stock and a felt pen and ask them to fold the cards and write their names on them, and then place the cards on their desks or on the table in front of them so that everyone can see their names. When all class participants have arrived, introduce yourself again and proceed to introduce the spiritual growth study *Concerning Prayer.*

Opening Worship

Call to Worship:

Almighty God, you have created us, called us, chosen us to be your people. We wait now to receive your guidance and blessing. Give us ears to hear, eyes to see, and hearts to respond to your love and grace. In the name of Christ we pray. Amen.

Hymn: #492, "Prayer Is the Soul's Sincere Desire,"
         The United Methodist Hymnal (verses 1, 2, and 3)

Litany: #743, "Psalm 8," *The United Methodist Hymnal*

Prayer: #495, "The Sufficiency of God,"
         The United Methodist Hymnal

Hymn: #492, "Prayer Is the Soul's Sincere Desire,"
         The United Methodist Hymnal (verses 4, 5, and 6)

Community-Building Exercise

Ask members of the study group to stand and form a circle. The leader stands in the center with a ball of yarn. The leader begins by stating her or his name and saying one thing she or he is thankful for. Holding the loose end of the yarn tightly, the leader tosses the ball to a member of the group, who in turn gives her or his name and states a different thing that he or she is thankful for. Wrapping the yarn tightly around his or her finger, the person tosses the ball to another member of the group. The procedure is repeated until all members of the group have been introduced and have had an opportunity to say what they are thankful for. The leader says a prayer of thanksgiving for the study group, the spiritual growth study, the mission of United Methodist Women, and the Church.

Introduction to the Study

The author of *Concerning Prayer*, Mary Kathryn Pearce, presents an excellent overview of the study in her introduction. Discuss the purpose of the study, the primary focus, and the various methods and definitions of prayer outlined in the introduction. Introduce the basic resources that have been prepared for the study; include additional resources available in the classroom and on the Internet. Emphasize that everyone needs a copy of the study book and a Bible. Participants will also need a notebook for the prayer book they are to create.

Discuss the expectations and guidelines for class participation. Explain your role as study leader and emphasize the importance of group participation in the learning process. Discuss how the activities and exercises in the study guide will enhance and enrich their learning experience. Allow time for questions or comments.

Group/Individual Activities

A. What is prayer?
  1. On a sheet of paper, write "Prayer is…." Complete this sentence with as many definitions of prayer as you can think of. Add to your list hymns found in *The United Methodist Hymnal* and scripture passages, especially from the Psalms, that help you understand what prayer is. You will have five minutes to complete your list.

  2. Form small groups of four or five and discuss your responses to the questions "What is prayer?" and "What do we do when we pray?"

  3. Compare your small group definitions of prayer. Have one person compile a list of group responses (eliminating duplicates). Be sure to include responses from everyone in the group. Using the compiled list, have members of the group print the combined responses on the 3" x 5" index cards provided. Create a prayer mobile for your group similar to the large prayer mobile displayed in the classroom. The large prayer mobile contains definitions of prayer found in the introduction and chapter one of the study book. Instructions for making a prayer mobile are on page 60 of the study guide. As a continuing exercise, add to the prayer mobiles as new definitions of prayer come to mind. During the course of the study, examine all of the mobiles displayed in the room.

B. Bible Study: The Prayer Life of Jesus

Jesus prayed and instructed his disciples to pray (Matthew 6:9-13; Luke 11:2-4). For Jesus, the priority of prayer is being in a right relationship with God: seek first the kingdom of God and righteousness. Jesus demonstrated this kind of relationship with God as a "life of living prayer." Scripture passages that describe Jesus' prayer life appear in the table below.

Jesus' Prayer Life

Matthew 11:25	Luke 6:12-16
Matthew 14:22-23	Luke 9:18
Mark 1:35	Luke 9:28-29
Mark 6:46	John 11:41b-42
Mark 14:36	John 12:27-28
Luke 5:15-16	John 17:1-5; 6-19; 20-26

1. Divide the study group into five or six smaller groups. Assign each group one or more of the scripture references listed in the table. Allow them ten minutes to study and discuss the selected passages.

2. As a whole group, discuss the following questions regarding Jesus' prayer life:

   a. Why do you think Jesus felt the need to pray?

   b. When did Jesus pray? What was happening at the time?

   c. Where was Jesus when he prayed?

   d. Who was with Jesus when he prayed?

   e. What kind of prayers did Jesus pray?

   f. What can we learn from Jesus' prayer life?

Learning Resources

A. Instructions for Creating a Prayer Mobile

Materials needed: large sheets of poster paper, 3" x 5" index cards, string or yarn, colored markers or felt pens, glue or masking tape.

On a large strip of poster paper, write "PRAYER IS...." Then print the responses on 3" x 5" index cards. Using masking tape or glue, attach an index card to one end of a piece of string or yarn. Then hang the other end of the string or yarn to the large strip of poster paper. Continue these steps until all index cards are hanging from the poster paper. Cut string or yarn in different lengths to create a mobile effect.

B. Definitions of Prayer Chart

Type	Definition and essential components
Invocation	The intentional reminder of the presence of God, bringing consciousness of the Divine presence. It is the act of inviting God to bring the awareness of Spirit into one's mind and soul.
Confession	The full and honest admission of one's sins and mistakes to God; honestly being sorry and sincerely requesting forgiveness.
Thanksgiving	The result of a grateful heart. There are five reasons for thanksgiving: Jesus Christ, all the means of grace, the joy and wonder of life, the gifts one receives, and people in our lives.
Petition	The act of asking God for those things needed for life and living. This prayer comes from the realization that one is dependent upon God for that which gives live and meaning to one's existence. As we pray this prayer, we give our wants and desires over to God, and ask that God's will be done.
Intercession	To offer a prayer of intercession is to lift the needs of the world to God for blessing and help. The naming of those in need is critical. God created us to be in relationship with others. We express that relationship through intercessory prayer. Honest Christ-like intercession is one of the most intense levels of communing with God.

Assignments for Session II

1. Read chapter two of the study book.
2. Using the definitions of prayer chart in the study guide, write a sentence prayer for each type of prayer defined in the chart.
3. Bring prayer books to session II. If participants have not started working on the book, time will be allotted during the session for them to work on it.
4. Ask for a volunteer to lead worship for session II.
5. Ask for three volunteers to portray the following spiritual icons: Dietrich Bonhoeffer, Hildegard of Bingin, and Martin Luther King, Jr.
6. Ask five volunteers to serve on a panel representing the following five spiritual icons:
   a. John Wesley
   b. St. Teresa of Avila
   c. Mohandas Gandhi
   d. Mother Teresa of Calcutta
   e. Henri Nouwen
7. Pray the prayers of John Wesley morning and evening.

   Morning: "Almighty and everlasting God, who has safely brought us to the beginning of this day; defend us in the same with thy mighty power; and grant that this day we fall into no sin; neither run into any kind of danger: but that all our doings may be ordered by thy governance, to do always what is righteous in thy sight, through Jesus Christ our Lord." Amen!

   Evening: "And now, as we lay ourselves down to sleep, take us into thy gracious protection and settle our spirits in quiet thoughts of thy glory." Amen!

Closing Worship

Moments of Silent Meditation (recorded music)

Prayer: #668, "Let Us Now Depart in Thy Peace," *The United Methodist Hymnal*

Let us now depart in thy peace, blessed Jesus. Send us to our homes with God's love in our hearts. Let not the busy world claim all our loyalties. Keep us ever mindful, dear Lord, of thee. Amen.

SESSION II

EMBRACING A LIFE OF PRAYER

Purpose

- To examine the prayer lives of past and contemporary spiritual icons
- To explore the different forms of prayer as a means to a disciplined prayer life
- To provide an opportunity for participants to apply what they've learned to their own prayer life development

Leader's Preparation for the Session

1. Equipment and materials needed for this session: VCR, TV monitor, newsprint, magic markers, 3" x 5" index cards, and yarn.

2. Add any new definitions of prayer found in chapter two to the large prayer mobile.

3. Secure as many images and works of the spiritual icons as possible. Create a mural of these images and place them on the wall. Enlarge quotes on prayer from the spiritual icons and display them on the mural or around the room.

4. Secure a set of *Reflection Prompters* (Service Center, Stock #1088, $2.95).

5. Prepare sheets of newsprint for a graffiti prayer wall.

6. Order the video *Questions of Faith – Series I: What Good Is Prayer?* Watch the video before class and select a segment (5 to 10 minutes) for viewing by participants. Purchase the video, part of Series I

(#2340), at https://secure.umcom.org/ecufilm. (*What Good Is Prayer* is part of a six-video set that can be purchased for a total of $50.)

Opening Worship

Hymn:	#352, "It's Me, It's Me, O Lord," *The United Methodist Hymnal*
Morning Prayers:	#677, "Listen, Lord (A Prayer)," *The United Methodist Hymnal*
	#681, "For Help for the Forthcoming Day," *The United Methodist Hymnal*
	#676, "For a New Day," *The United Methodist Hymnal*
Prayers for Persons in Mission and Mission Projects:	*2004 Prayer Calendar*
Hymn:	#404, "Every Time I Feel the Spirit," *The United Methodist Hymnal*

Introduction to Session II

Briefly review the concepts and discussion points from the previous session. Respond to any questions or concerns regarding session I. State the purpose of today's session. On newsprint, outline the key points in chapter two of the study book that will guide today's discussion. Mention other resources in the room that will also be useful for the session.

Group/Individual Activities

A. Create a graffiti prayer wall of the prayers of invocation, confession, thanksgiving petition, and intercession written by class members as an assignment for this session.

B. View a five- to ten-minute segment of the video *Questions of Faith – Series I: What Good Is Prayer?*

  1. Reflect on your own questions regarding faith and prayer.

2. On a sheet of paper or in a notebook, write your reflections on the following questions.
   a. What does prayer mean to me?
   b. What good is prayer?
3. Turn to the person next to you and share your responses.

C. Optional activity: After viewing the video *Questions of Faith – Series I: What Good Is Prayer?* ask for five volunteers to form a panel. The study group leader may serve as moderator. Ask each panelist to respond to the following questions: (1) What does prayer mean to you? (2) What good is prayer?

D. Visit by spiritual icons: Hildegard of Bingin, Dietrich Bonhoeffer, and Martin Luther King, Jr. Arrange for these individuals to make their appearance in the classroom to tell their stories at different times during the session. Study-group members who volunteered to portray these individuals will be given five minutes each for their presentations. During each monologue, study-group participants will be listening for clues to the secret to a devout life of prayer.

The three class members who volunteered to portray Martin Luther King, Jr., Hildegard of Bingin, and Dietrich Bonhoeffer should dress according to the period in which they lived (Hildegard of Bingin can wear a head scarf). The outline below can be used for preparing the narrative monologues. The narration should not exceed five minutes.

1. Identify yourself.
2. Relate important events in early childhood.
3. Relate important events in adulthood.
4. Explain the role of prayer in your life.
5. Cite important works published.

E. Panel of visiting spiritual icons: St. Teresa of Avila, Mother Teresa of Calcutta, Mohandas Gandhi, John Wesley, Henri Nouwen. Panelists should be dressed according to the time period in which they lived. A sheet or robe may be worn as a costume. The moderator will introduce each member of the panel and then ask them a series of questions. The script below can be used to help panelists prepare for the discussion.

Script

Moderator *(addressing St. Teresa of Avila, Mohandas Gandhi, Henri Nouwen, John Wesley, and Mother Teresa):*
What does prayer mean to you?

Order of Responses: St. Teresa, Gandhi, Nouwen, Wesley, Mother Teresa

Moderator: How do you experience the Spirit of God?

Order of Responses: Gandhi, Nouwen, Wesley, Mother Teresa, St. Teresa

Moderator: Describe your process for growing into a life of prayer.

Order of Responses: Nouwen, Wesley, Mother Teresa, St. Teresa, Gandhi

Moderator: How does prayer change peoples' lives?

Order of Responses: Wesley, Mother Teresa, St. Teresa, Gandhi, Nouwen

Moderator: Describe a formula you use for living a life of prayer.

Order of Responses: Mother Teresa, St. Teresa, Gandhi, Nouwen, Wesley

As they are making their presentations, listen for definitions of prayer and for the formula for embracing a life of prayer each describes. Then respond to the following questions:

1. What formula(s) or aid(s) do you use for living a life of prayer?
2. Identify spiritual icons in your own life journey. Include people from United Methodist Women, past or present.
3. Turn to your neighbor and share your answers to these questions.
4. Add these names to the spiritual icon mural on the wall in the classroom.

After asking the class if there are any additional questions for the members of the panel, the moderator then closes the discussion by thanking the panelists and making appropriate closing remarks.

F. Creating a Prayer Book

   1. From magazines cut out pictures of peaceful nature scenes, children, or animals, and paste them in a notebook. When you come across a wonderful quotation on prayer, copy it into the book using multicolored pens. Paste the picture or photo opposite the prayer. *The United Methodist Hymnal* and the Psalms are good sources of prayers.

   2. Spend about 15 minutes on your prayer books.

   3. Return to your seats or find a quiet place in the classroom where you can have some solitude. Reread the prayers you have written in your prayer book. Look at the accompanying pictures and meditate, pray, and listen to God speaking to you. The leader will tell you when to end the silence.

Assignments for Session III

1. Read chapters three and four.

2. Begin and end the day with prayer. Morning and evening prayers of John Wesley are printed on page 62 of the study guide for your use.

3. Ask a volunteer to lead worship for session III.

4. Ask volunteers to learn the words and liturgical movements to Psalm 100 for the worship on the last day of the study. See the section on praying with words and movement on page 75 of the study guide.

Closing Prayer

Prayers of Intercession:

God created us to be in relationship with others. Intercessory prayer is one way to express that relationship. In 1 John 4:20-21 we read these words:

If anyone says, "I love God," yet hates his brother, he is a liar. For anyone who does not love his brother, whom he has seen, cannot love God, whom he has not seen. And he has given us this command: Whoever loves God must also love his brother.

This passage from 1 John tells us that the act of loving God naturally implies that we love one another. Douglas V. Steere, in *Dimensions of Prayer*, reminds us that intercession is the most intensely social act that the human being is capable of.[1]

(After each prayer, the leader may conclude: "Lord, in your mercy." All may respond: "Hear our prayer.")

Together, let us pray for:
- the members of this study group
- those who suffer and those in trouble
- the concerns of this community
- the world, its people, and its leaders
- the missionaries, deaconesses, and other persons in mission here at home and around the world
- the church and her mission in the world
- United Methodist Women and women who are in mission around the world
- the communion of saints.

---

[1] Douglas V. Steere, *Dimensions of Prayer* (Nashville: The Upper Room General Board of Discipleship, 1997), p. 80.

SESSION III

THE LORD'S PRAYER AND PATTERNS OF PRAYING

Purpose

- To compare the Matthew and Luke texts of the Lord's Prayer
- To examine the content and meaning of the Lord's Prayer
- To examine different patterns of praying
- To provide an opportunity for participants to use one or more patterns of praying in developing their personal prayer lives

Leader's Preparation for the Session

1. Equipment and materials needed for this session: newsprint, magic markers, 3" x 5" index cards, and yarn.

2. Add any new definitions of prayer found in chapters three and four to the large prayer mobile.

3. Make a poster of the three versions of the Lord's Prayer in *The United Methodist Hymnal*, #894, #895, and #896.

4. Reproduce the Lord's Prayer table on page 72 of the study guide as a handout for study-group members. The Matthew and Luke texts of the Lord's Prayer are printed side by side for ease of comparison.

5. One of the group/individual activities suggested for this session involves finger-walking a paper labyrinth. PAXworks (Works of Peace) offers a free printable paper labyrinth with instructions on their website: http://www.paxworks.com. On the home page, click "free - printable labyrinths." You will be directed to a page that asks you to choose the labyrinth size you want to print. The labyrinth from PAXworks is a scale replica of an ancient labyrinth built into the stone floor of Chartres Cathedral in France during the 12th century. Make copies of the labyrinth and instructions for each participant or assign this task to a member of the class.

Opening Worship

Music: "The Lord's Prayer"
                       (recorded music, solo or unison singing)

Prayer: #607, A Covenant Prayer in the Wesleyan Tradition,
                       The United Methodist Hymnal

Hymn: #496, "Sweet Hour of Prayer,"
                       The United Methodist Hymnal

Introduction to Session III

Briefly review the concepts and discussion points from the previous session. Answer any questions or concerns regarding session II. State the purpose of today's session. On newsprint, outline the key points in chapters three and four of the study book that will guide today's discussion. Mention other resources in the room that will also be useful for this session.

Group/Individual Activities

A. Spend 15 minutes on your prayer book or journal.

B. Add to the prayer mobile any new definitions of prayer that you thought of or read during your preparation for this session. Also, add to the prayer mural names of other spiritual icons who have come to mind.

C. Bible Study: The Anatomy of the Lord's Prayer

   1. Read the handout of the Matthew and Luke texts of the Lord's Prayer. One member of the group will read aloud the Matthew text. Another group member will read aloud the Luke passage.

   2. Discuss the differences between the two texts. What is the cultural and social context in which Jesus instructs the disciples to pray this prayer?

   3. The Anatomy of the Lord's Prayer. Divide the class into seven small groups. Assign each group one of the seven structural segments of the Lord's Prayer as outlined in chapter three. Ask each group to discuss their assigned segment. Designate one person in each group to take notes and report back to the entire group.

4. Elements of prayer include: adoration of God; longing for God's reign; daily needs; relational healing; strength for the spiritual journey.

    a. Which elements of prayer are easy or difficult for you? Why?

    b. What should be the relationship between the Lord's Prayer and your own prayer?

    c. How do you usually pray?

    d. At times have you felt that God is not listening? What do you do then?

D. Meditation and Prayer

Meditation is a very important dimension of prayer. Often called "mental prayer," meditation is conscious yet non-vocal communication with God. During the process of meditating, our minds focus on a subject or thought. When we meditate while praying, the focus is on God. Other subjects of meditation may include a scripture passage, a line of prayer, a stanza of a hymn, or an object found in nature. During meditation, we can invite God to be present in our thoughts and our actions.

We can use a number of meditation techniques to develop a deeper prayer life. (See the meditation techniques table on page 77 of the study guide). Select from the list one or more forms of meditation to practice during this session. Then respond to the following questions:

1. Upon what did you focus?

2. Did your thoughts merge with God's thoughts?

3. How can you be more meditative in your prayers?

E. Finger-Walking a Personal Labyrinth

Walking the labyrinth is another form of meditation. Each walk through the labyrinth is different. The labyrinth is a way of opening ourselves to what God shows us on the journey. Read the brief history and guidelines for walking the labyrinth. If the labyrinth is printed on 8" x 11" paper, you will have to tape the labyrinth together.

You are now ready for a pilgrimage that will lead to a deeper spiritual awareness of the presence of God. Follow the "Finger-Walking a Personal Labyrinth" instructions from the PAXworks Internet printout sheet to begin the journey. Your study leader will tell you when to bring this exercise to a close.

Learning Resources

A. The Lord's Prayer

The two texts for the prayer Jesus taught his disciples are printed in the table below (New Revised Standard Version).

Matthew 6:9-13	Luke 11:2-4
"Our Father in heaven,	"Father,
hallowed be your name,	hallowed be your name,
your kingdom come,	your kingdom come.
your will be done	
on earth as it is in heaven.	
Give us this day our daily	Give us each day our daily
bread.	bread.
And forgive us our debts,	And forgive us our sins,
as we also have forgiven	for we ourselves forgive
our debtor.	everyone indebted to us.
And do not bring us to the	And do not bring us to the
time of trial,	time of trial."
but rescue us from the evil one."	

B. Patterns of Praying

Prayer increases our awareness of God. There are many patterns of prayer. Whether we are praying a Psalm, the Lord's Prayer, a scripture, personal and intercessory prayers, or our favorite hymn, we are in prayer. Likewise, our journal time can serve as an opportunity for writing prayers. While there are various ways to pray or talk with God, we generally use the method that best fits our needs and circumstances. The table below lists the various methods or patterns of praying mentioned in the study book.

Patterns/Methods	Illustration
Singing Prayers	Songs, hymns, spirituals, gospel music, etc. Sing or listen. Let the music go deep. Dance if the Spirit moves you.
Praying the Psalms	The Psalms can be read, chanted or sung. Try writing your own psalm of praise, lament, danger, or victory.
Cultural Prayer Patterns	Prayer patterns vary by culture, congregation, age group, etc. What are the patterns in your culture? What patterns have you experienced in other cultures?
Nature Prayers	Embracing all of God's creation. Think about those moments in nature when awe of God's world inspired you.
Praying in Solitude	Solitude can be structured through journaling, using the written prayers of others, looking at nature, silent meditation, guided prayer tapes, listening to music, praying during a walk or run, or creating a worship center.

Intercessory Prayers	Praying for others. Keep a list and write down the answers to your prayers.
Fasting	Fasting is the act of temporarily giving up something that is very important to us in order that we may use the time normally given to that thing for prayer and reflection. Intercessory prayer can be greatly strengthen by fasting. Check with your doctor before giving up food.
Corporate Prayers	Prayers of the gathered church and the community of believers are powerful for affirming and teaching our faith. We are not alone.
Breath Prayers	Short, one-sentence prayers that may be said in one breath as we breathe in and out. This can be done during a focused time of deeply relaxed meditation or throughout the day.
Movement Prayers	Liturgical movement can be performed in a congregation or small group, or alone. Very simple movements can bring the prayer of song into the heart.

C. Praying with Words and Movement:[2] Psalm 100

1. Make a joyful noise to the Lord, all the lands!	Starting position: Stand facing forward with hands at sides. Step forward on right foot, at the same time focusing eyes upward and raising both arms, palms facing body. Left hand overlapping right hand, pass hands close to mouth, lift arms high, and then open them to denote "all the lands."
2. Serve the Lord with gladness!	Half kneel, right foot forward. Lower arms with outstretched hands in position of giving. Focus still upward. Be glad.
Come into his presence with singing!	Rise to standing. Take two steps forward, at the same time assuming arm position and movement of first line. End with hands not separated, with right hand slightly higher than left. Focus still upward.
3. Know that the Lord is God!	Continue in same position except clench fists in a controlled movement. Lower arms slightly, raise again for emphasis.
It is he that made us, and we are his;	Bring right hand down, pointing to but not touching self. Lower and reach forward with left hand, palm up (to include all people). On "we are his," raise both hands high and fairly wide.
we are his people, and the sheep of his pasture.	Hold that position, then on "sheep" drop to half-kneeling position and look down on "pasture" as hands move out to side and back together with palms down. On "his" (last line) focus upward.

[2] Adapted from Doris Peterson, *Worship with Words and Movement* (Women's Division of Christian Service, Board of Missions, The United Methodist Church, New York, 1970), p. 19.

4. Enter his gates with thanksgiving,	Rise to standing. Take two steps forward, hands loosely clasped in front of chest. Look upward, then downward.
and his courts with praise!	Take one more step forward. Raise hands high and separate them about shoulder width.
Give thanks to him, bless his name!	Drop to a half kneel. Bring hands down and clasp them loosely in front of chest. Focus upward. On "bless his name," raise hands upward, right hand slightly above left.
5. For the Lord is good;	Rise to standing. Stand tall. Raise clasped hands high and press them together tightly. Focus upward.
his steadfast love endures for ever, and his faithfulness to all generations.	Movement continuous: circle arms outward, sideward, downward, crossing them in front of body and continuing until they are stretched high. On "faithfulness," bring arms forward, downward shoulder-high with left palm up, right palm down. Move right hand to right side and back to denote "all generations." Finish with right palm up. Slowly raise arms high and separate them somewhat. Hold.

D. Meditation Techniques

Meditation is a spiritual and religious practice that helps us deepen our understanding and awareness of the sacredness of life. Meditation techniques have existed for thousands of years and are often used as a tool for developing a disciplined prayer life. As we practice the techniques of meditation, our minds and bodies are relaxed, and our souls are nourished and open to the presence of the Holy Spirit. We experience a feeling of calm, peace, and tranquility.

According to recent medical studies, meditation has proven health benefits. Research conducted by the Mayo Clinic links the daily practice of meditation to a reduction in tension, stress, and the risk of heart disease.[3] The following table lists some ways to meditate, relax, and nourish the soul and prepare for prayer.

Meditation techniques are the outward actions which have been developed in many religious traditions. When we use any technique and contemplate Christ, we deepen our Christian walk.

Activity	Description
Sitting quietly in a room alone	Think about all the things you are thankful for, then offer a prayer of thanksgiving to God.
Breathing exercises	Relaxation breathing can calm and help you focus. Breathe deeply and slowly, become aware of each breath.
Yoga	This form of meditation in motion is an ancient practice from India that incorporates proper breathing, movement, and posture.
Tai chi	Tai chi is an ancient Chinese martial art. It involves gentle, circular movements combined with deep breathing. It is described today as a form of "moving meditation."
Walking	Walking is an excellent way to relax and meditate with nature. Observe your surroundings, look at God's creative powers in the universe. Whisper prayers of thanksgiving and gratitude for all of creation. A labyrinth walk is a meditative journey.

[3] "Meditation: Calming your mind, body, and spirit," at http://www.MayoClinic.com.

Listening to music	Select music that has a calming, relaxing effect on you. Playing a musical instrument can also be a good way to center yourself and meditate.
Journaling	Writing your innermost thoughts in a journal while meditating or during moments of solitude is a meaningful activity.
Using written prayers of others	Using the prayers of others, hymns, or the Psalms, can help create a meditative mood.
Reflection prompters	This set of 24 cards consists of quotes and prayers that can be used for meditation, comfort, and challenge. Available through Service Center (Stock #01088, $2.95).

E. The Labyrinth: Walking Your Spiritual Journey

A labyrinth symbolizes the journey to the center of one's self. Found in many cultures and traditions, labyrinths date as far back as 3500 BC. The early labyrinths were built on the grounds of monasteries and on the floors of the great cathedrals in France. The following websites provide information about this ancient form of walking meditation:

http://www.thedome.org/SpiritQuest/SacredSpace/labyrinth/labmid.html
http://www.paxworks.com
http://anchorageuuf.org/Labyrinth.html
http://www.creativespirit.net/MabArt/labyrinth.htm
http://www.labyrinthproject.com/designs.html

Assignments for Session IV

1. Read chapter five.
2. Begin and end the day with prayer.
3. Class members who volunteered to learn the words and movements to Psalm 100 will participate in the opening worship for this last session.

Closing Prayer

Dear God, through Jesus the Christ, we have met you and experienced your great mercy and love. We thank you for this gift and for every new thing we have discovered today that adds to our knowledge and understanding of your love, joy, and peace. Teach us, O God, how to pray as Jesus taught the disciples. *(Here members of the class may pray in unison the Lord's Prayer in their native language.)*

SESSION IV

PRAYING INTO THE TOMORROWS

Purpose

- To introduce the principles for a life centered in prayer
- To explore the mystery of prayer and its implications for our lives
- To engage participants in a discussion of the relationship between private prayer and corporate worship
- To examine the different ways to pray into tomorrow

Leader's Preparation for the Session

1. On newsprint, write the learning points on prayer in chapter five of the study book.

2. Add any new definitions of prayer from chapter five to the prayer mobile.

3. Display prayer posters featuring praying hands, adults praying, and children praying. The following websites are a good source for prayer posters: http://www.allposters.com and http://www.art.com. Also search for "prayer posters" at http://www.google.com.

Opening Worship

Worship in Word and Movement: Psalm 100

Hymn: #126, "Sing Praise to God Who Reigns Above,"
          The United Methodist Hymnal

Prayer: #329, "Prayer to the Holy Spirit," A Native American
          Prayer, *The United Methodist Hymnal*

Introduction to Session IV

Briefly review the concepts and discussion points from the previous session. Answer any questions or concerns regarding session III. State the purpose of today's session and outline on newsprint the key points in chapter five of the study book that will guide today's discussion. Mention other resources in the room that will also be useful for this session.

Group/Individual Activities

A. Spend about 15 minutes working on your prayer books at the beginning of the session.

B. Add any new names of spiritual icons to the mural; add new definitions of prayer to the prayer mobile.

C. Bible Study: Why Do We Pray?

In chapter five of the study book, Mary Kathryn Pearce quotes William James, the American philosopher, on prayer. James says, "The reason why we pray is simply that we cannot help praying." The desire to pray is with us as we enter into this life. Mary Kathryn Pearce believes that the desire to pray is innate, but certain aspects of praying have to be learned. What do you believe is the reason we pray? Turn to a neighbor and discuss your response to this question.

The following biblical passages, Matthew 26:36-44, Luke 11:5-13, and Luke 18:1-8, provide insights into why and how we should pray. Divide the study group into three smaller groups and assign each group one of the three scripture references. Allow 20 minutes for the groups to read, discuss, and answer the questions related to the passage.

1. Matthew 26:36-44: Jesus Prays at Gethsemane

   The ultimate example of opening the heart and soul to God is the prayer Jesus prayed at Gethsemane on the night before his crucifixion.

   a. What did Jesus ask of God?

   b. What lessons for our lives today can we draw from Jesus' prayer?

2. Luke 11:5-13: Jesus' Teaching on Prayer

   In Luke 11:5-13, Jesus interprets the Lord's Prayer by telling the disciples the parable of the friends at midnight.

   a. What does Jesus say about why we pray?

   b. What is required of us when we pray?

   c. Do we need any special prayer techniques when we pray to God?

3. Luke 18:1-8: Parable of the Persistent Widow

   The parable of the persistent widow is an example of answered prayer for those who pray without ceasing.

   a. We pray for something and it is fulfilled. We pray for something else and nothing happens or things get worse. Does God answer all prayers?

   b. How does this parable help us respond to the above question?

D. Precepts of Praying

   Mary Kathryn Pearce sets forth principles that lead to a life centered in prayer. Discuss these principles in small groups. Then return to the larger group for a time of sharing.

E. Private Prayer and Corporate Worship

   1. How does praying in solitude differ from praying in a group?

   2. Suggest different ways people pray during corporate worship.

3. Are you comfortable praying in a corporate setting? If you do, what helps you feel this way? If you don't, why not?

4. Using the breath prayer, pray corporately but silently. Afterward, briefly share your experience.

F. Have the group members write in their notebooks a prayer plan that reflects what they would like to incorporate into their prayer lives.

Learning Resource

The Breath Prayer

The breath prayer is a very short prayer, usually only one sentence long. This form of prayer comes from the Hebrew word *ruach*, which means "wind," "breath," or "spirit." Breath prayers are a form of intercessory prayer that can be used not only in our daily routine but also in times of frustration, anxiety, fear, and distress (e.g., during surgery or illness). Breath prayers help us to "pray without ceasing." This type of prayer can be most meaningful in praying for another person, forming prayer chains, and building community.

In his book *Into the Light*,[4] Ron Delbene outlines several steps that one can use in creating breath prayers. The following is an adaptation of Delbene's five-step, self-directed program for creating breath prayers:

1. Sit quietly in a comfortable position and be still and calm. Close your eyes and imagine that you are in the presence of God. Recalling a favorite passage of scripture can help prepare you for being in the moment.

2. Imagine that God is calling you by name. Hear God asking you: "[Your name], what do you want?'

3. Respond to God with whatever comes honestly from your heart. Ask yourself: What do I really want that will make me whole? It could be peace of mind or healing from an illness. Your response will be at the heart of your prayer.

---

[4] Ron Delbene, *Into the Light* (Nashville: Upper Room Books, 1988).

4. Choose your favorite name for God: Jesus, Christ, Lord, Father, God, Creator, Spirit, Mother God, etc.

5. Combine your name for God with your responses to God's question, "What do you want?" and you will have your own personal breath prayer. Write the prayer down and use it several times during the day. Let the prayer become part of your daily life. Repeat it several times as you breathe in and out.

Examples

- What I want is peace; my name for God is Lord; and my breath prayer is: "Lord, let me know your peace."

- What I want is God's presence; my name for God is Creator God; and my breath prayer is "Creator God, lead me to the light of Christ."

Pray your breath prayer as you breathe in and out. It should become as natural as inhaling and exhaling.

Closing Worship

Call to Worship: #477, "For Illumination,"
The United Methodist Hymnal

Open wide the window of our spirit, O Lord, and fill us full of light; open wide the door of our hearts, that we may receive and entertain thee with all our powers of adoration and love. Amen.

Reading for Reflection:

I call to you, O Lord, from my quiet darkness. Show me your mercy and love. Let me see your face, hear your voice, and touch the hem of your cloak. I want to love you, be with you, speak to you, and simply stand in your presence. But I cannot make it happen. Pressing my eyes against my hands is not praying, and reading about your presence is not living in it.

But there is that moment in which you will come to me, as you did to your fearful disciples, and say, "Do not be afraid; it is I." Let that moment come soon, O Lord. And if you want to delay it, then make me patient. Amen.

From *A Cry for Mercy* by Henri J. M. Nouwen (New York: Doubleday, 1981).

Hymn: #430, "O Master, Let Me Walk with Thee,"
          The United Methodist Hymnal

Benediction:

And now may the spirit which was in Jesus Christ be in us, enabling us to know God's will and empowering us to do God's will. Now and forevermore. Amen.

Bibliography

A selected bibliography compiled by Ernest Rubinstein, librarian of the Ecumenical Library, The Interchurch Center, New York, N.Y.

Used copies of out-of-print books and of many books in print are available through the search engines: http://www.bookfinder.com; http://www.addall.com; http://www.alibris.com, Amazon.com, and BarnesandNoble.com. Thanks are due the librarians of Union Theological Seminary and New York Theological Seminary for providing access to their book stacks.

Biblical Resources for Prayer

In the New Testament alone, readers might consult the following passages for prayer instructions: Matthew 6:5-8; Mark 11:22-28; Luke 11:1-13, 18:1-14; Colossians 4:2-4; James 5:13-18; 1 Peter 3:12. Perhaps there has been no more influential source of prayer from the Old Testament than the Psalms; and no more widely known and practiced New Testament prayer than the Lord's Prayer.

General

Ballantine, Samuel. *Prayer in the Hebrew Bible: The Drama of Divine Human Encounter*. Minneapolis: Fortress, 1993. 311 p. $21.00

Dowd, Sharyn Echols. *Prayer, Power and the Problem of Suffering: Mark 11:22-25 in the Context of Markan Theology*. Atlanta: Society of Biblical Literature, 1988. 186 p. $12.95

Fosdick, Harry Emerson. *The Meaning of Prayer*. Nashville: Abingdon, 2003. 32 p. $14.00 [first published 1915]

Fosua, Abena Safiyah. *Jesus and Prayer*. Nashville: Abingdon Press, 2002. 104 p. $8.50

Koenig, John. *Rediscovering New Testament Prayer: Boldness and Blessing in the Name of Jesus.* Harrisburg, Penn.: Morehouse, 1992. 203 p. $15.95

Meehan, Bridget Mary. *Praying with the Women of the Bible.* Liguori, Mo.: Liguori, 1998. 159 p. $12.95

Miller, Patrick. *They Cried to the Lord: Form and Theology of Biblical Prayer.* Minneapolis: Fortress, 1994. 464 p. $28.00

Ramsey, Michael. *Be Still and Know: A Study in the Life of Prayer.* Boston: Cowley, 1993. 108 p. $9.95 [first published 1983]

Roberts, Howard W. *Praying Like Jesus.* Cleveland: Pilgrim Press, 1999. 175 p. $15.95

Psalms and the Lord's Prayer

Brueggemann, Walter. *Praying the Psalms.* Winona, Minn.: St. Mary's Press, 1993. 72 p. $5.95

Endres, John C. and Elizabeth Liebert. *A Retreat with the Psalms: Resources for Personal and Communal Prayer.* Mahwah, N.J.: Paulist, 2001. 254 p. $16.95

Kalajainen, Larry R. *Psalms for the Journey: The Lord's Song in Ordinary Time.* Nashville: Upper Room Books, 1996. 128 p. $10.00

Lewis, Thomas. *Finding God: Praying the Psalms in Times of Depression.* Louisville, Ky.: Westminster, 2002. 146 p. $7.00

Bondi, Roberta. *A Place to Pray: Reflections on the Lord's Prayer.* Nashville: Abingdon, 1998. 144 p. $17.00

Coburn, John B. *Deliver Us from Evil: the Prayer of Our Lord*. San Francisco: HarperSanFrancisco, 1984. 96 p. $4.95

Crosby, Michael H. *Thy Will Be Done: Praying the* Our Father *as Subversive Activity.* Maryknoll, N.Y.: Orbis Books, 1977. 254 p. Out of print.

Douglas-Klotz, Neil. *Prayers of the Cosmos: Meditations on the Aramaic Words of Jesus*. San Francisco: Harper & Row, 1990. 112 p. $13.00

Mulholland, James. *Praying Like Jesus: The Lord's Prayer in a Culture of Prosperity.* San Francisco: HarperSanFrancisco, 2001. 133 p. $14.95

Raphael, Pierre. *God Behind Bars: A Prison Chaplain Reflects on the Lord's Prayer*. Mahway, N.J.: Paulist, 1999. 144 p. $10.95

Stevenson, Kenneth. *Abba, Father: Understanding and Using the Lord's Prayer*. Harrisburg, Penn.: Morehouse, 2001. 202 p. $17.95

Studies on Prayer

James, William. *The Varieties of Religious Experience*. Touchstone Books, 1997. 416 p. $8.00 [first published 1902]

Perspectives on Prayer. Edited by Fraser Watts. London: SPCK, 2001. 128 p. $15.00

Prayer from Alexander to Constantine: A Critical Anthology. Edited by Mark Kiley. New York: Routledge, 1997. 332 p. $29.95

Praying with Power. Edited by Joe Aldred. New York: Continuum, 2000. 160 p. $16.95

Guides to Praying

Bondi, Roberta C. *In Ordinary Time: Healing the Wounds of the Heart.* Nashville: Abingdon, 1996. 205 p. $17.00

Castelli, Jim. *How I Pray.* New York: Ballantine, 1994. 188 p. $15.00

Clare, Mary. *Encountering the Depths*: *Prayer, Solitude, and Contemplation.* Harrisburg, Penn. Morehouse, 1995. 112 p. $9.95

Fiand, Barbara. *Prayer and the Quest for Healing: Our Personal Transformation and Cosmic Responsibility.* New York: Crossroad, 1999. 178 p. $14.95

Forest, Jim. *Praying with Icons.* Maryknoll, N.Y.: Orbis Books, 1997. 171 p. $16.00

Grumbach, Doris. *Presence of Absence: On Prayer and an Epiphany.* Boston: Beacon, 1998. 126 p. $18.00

Hamlin, Rick. *Finding God on the A-Train*: *A Journey into Prayer.* San Francisco: HarperSanFrancisco, 1997. 152 p. $10.00

Keating, Charles J. *Who We Are Is How We Pray: Matching Personality and Spirituality.* Mystic, Conn.: Twenty-Third Publications, 1987. 147 p. $9.95

Keating, Thomas. *Intimacy with God: An Introduction to Centering Prayer.* New York: Crossroad, 1994. 167 p. $13.95

Killinger, John. *Beginning Prayer.* Nashville, Tenn.: Upper Room, 1993. 107 p. $9.00

McClain, George. *Claiming All Things for God: Prayer, Discernment and Ritual for Social Change.* Nashville: Abingdon, 1998. 152 p. $13.00

McPherson, C. W. *Keeping Silence: Christian Practices for Entering Stillness*. Harrisburg, Pa.: Morehouse, 2002. 96 p. $12.95

Meehan, Bridget Mary and Regina Madonna Oliver. *Praying with a Passionate Heart*. Liguori, Mo.: Liguori, 1999. 110 p. $12.95

Merton, Thomas. *New Seeds of Contemplation*. New York: New Directions, 1974. 297 p. $12.95 [first published 1962]

Norris, Kathleen. *The Cloister Walk*. New York: Berkley Publishing Group, 1996. 385 p. $12.95

Nouwen, Henri J. M. *With Open Hands*. Notre Dame, Ind.: Ave Maria Press, 1995. 132 p. $12.95

Pennington, Basil. *Centering Prayer: Renewing an Ancient Christian Prayer Form*. New York: Doubleday, 1982. 188 p. $9.95

Proctor-Smith, Marjorie. *Praying with our Eyes Open: Engendering Feminist Liturgical Prayer*. Nashville: Abingdon, 1995. 176 p. $17.00

Rhude, Beth E. *Live the Questions Now: The Interior Life*. [New York]: Women's Division, Board of Global Ministries, United Methodist Church, 1980. 168 p. Out of print [many used copies available through http://www.bookfinder.com].

Steere, Douglas. *Dimensions of Prayer: Cultivating a Relationship with God*. Nashville: Upper Room Books, 2002. 128 p. $12.00 [first published 1962]

Vennard, Jane. *Embracing the World: Praying for Justice and Peace*. San Francisco: Jossey-Bass, 2003. 145 p. $18.95

Wuellner, Flora Slossan. *Prayer and Our Bodies*. Nashville: Abingdon, 1987. 144 p. $12.00

Methodist Traditions of Prayer

Council of Bishops of the United Methodist Church. *Vital Congregations, Faithful Disciples: Vision for the Church.* Nashville: Graded Press, 1990. 160 p. Out of print.

DeSilva, David A. *Praying with John Wesley.* Nashville: Discipleship Resources, 2001. 48 p. $7.95

Job, Reuben. *A Wesleyan Spiritual Reader.* Nashville: Abingdon, 1997. 216 p. $15.00

Kimbrough, S. T. *Lost in Wonder: Charles Wesley, the Meaning of His Hymns Today.* Nashville: Upper Room, 1987. 176 p.

Knight, Henry H. *Eight Life-Enriching Practices of United Methodists.* Nashville: Abingdon, 2001. 136 p. $6.50

McMullen, Michael. *Hearts Aflame: Prayers of Susanna, John, and Charles Wesley.* London: SPCK, 2000. 144 p. $9.00 [distributed by Pilgrim Press, Cleveland, Ohio]

Ecumenical and Interfaith Prayer

Bowman, Gail. *Praying the Sacred in Secular Settings.* St. Louis, Mo.: Chalice, 2000. 111 p. $14.99

Carmody, Denise Lardner and John Tully Carmody. *Prayer in World Religions.* Maryknoll, N.Y.: Orbis Books, 1990. 168 p. $14.00

Castro, Emilio. *When We Pray Together.* Geneva: World Council of Churches, 1989. 86 p. $8.50

Cox, Harvey. *Common Prayers: Faith, Family, and a Christian's Journey through the Jewish Year.* Boston: Houghton Mifflin, 2001. 305 p. $13.00

Foerster, L. Annie. *For Praying Out Loud: Interfaith Prayers for Public Occasions.* Boston: Skinner House, 2003. 150 p. $14.00

Green, Michael and Coleman Barks. *The Illuminated Prayer: The Five-Times Prayer of the Sufi.* New York: Ballantine Publishing, 2000. 144 p. $18.95

Praying with Jewish Tradition. Compiled by Elias Kopciowski. Grand Rapids, Mich.: Eerdmans, 1997. 134 p. $9.95

Shannon, Maggie Oman. *The Way We Pray: Prayer Practices from around the World.* York Beach, Maine: Conari Press, 2001. 220 p. $15.95

Steere, Douglas. *Prayer in the Contemporary World.* Wallingsford, Penn: Pendle Hill, 1990. 32 p. $4.00 [free at http://www.pendlehill.org/pendle_hill_pamphlets.htm]

Prayer Anthologies

An African Prayer Book. Edited by Bishop Desmond Tutu. New York: Doubleday, 1995. 139 p. $21.00

Barclay, William. *A Barclay Prayer Book.* Louisville, Ky: Westminster Press, 2003. 350 p. $14.95

The Book of Mystical Chapters: Meditations on the Soul's Ascent, from the Desert Fathers and other Early Christian Contemplatives. Translated and introduced by John Anthony McGuckin. Boston: Shambhala, 2002. 215 p. $19.95

Brueggemann, Walter. *Awed to Heaven, Rooted in Earth: Prayers of Walter Brueggemann.* Minneapolis: Fortress, 2003. 176 p. $14.00

Conversations with God: Two Centuries of Prayers by African Americans. Edited by James Melvin Washington. New York: HarperCollins, 1994. 347 p. $15.00

Dare to Dream: A Prayer and Worship Anthology from around the World. Edited by Geoffrey Duncan. London: Fount Paperbacks, 1995. 250 p. Out of print.

Every Eye Beholds You: A World Treasury of Prayer. Edited by Thomas J. Craughwell. New York: Harcourt Brace, 1998. 320 p. $25.00

The Flowering of the Soul: A Book of Prayers by Women. Edited by Lucinda Vardey. Boston: Beacon Press, 2002. 400 p. $16.00

Gift of Prayer: A Treasury of Personal Prayer from the World's Spiritual Traditions. New York: Continuum, 1997. 274 p. $12.95

L'Engle, Madeleine and Luci Shaw. *A Prayerbook for Spiritual Friends: Partners in Prayer.* Minneapolis: Augsburg, 1999. 96 p. $10.99

Peace Prayers: Meditations, Affirmations, Invocations, Poems, and Prayers for Peace. Edited by the staff of Harper San Francisco. San Francisco: HarperSanFrancisco, 1992. 144 p. $10.00

Prayers Encircling the World: An International Anthology. Louisville, Ky.: Westminster John Knox Press, 1998. 278 p. $15.00

2000 Years of Prayer. Compiled by Michael Counsell. Harrisburg, Penn.: Morehouse, 2002. 672 p. $24.00

WomanPrayers: Prayers from Women from throughout History and around the World. San Francisco: HarperSanFrancisco, 2003. 224 p. $19.95

About the Authors

Reverend Mary Kathryn Pearce is an elder in The United Methodist Church and is a member of the Illinois Great Rivers Conference. Presently, she is appointed as the lead pastor at Prospect UMC in Dunlap, Illinois, located on the northern edge of Peoria.

Mary Kathryn has been related to Schools of Christian Mission for over twenty years. She has served as dean of her conference school and has taught in numerous conference and regional schools. In addition, she has written program materials for UMW and articles for *Response* magazine, served as a presenter for Assembly, and directed spiritual growth retreats in various districts and conferences of the UMC. Mary Kathryn has been a member of the General Commission on the Status and Role of Women and has been adjunct faculty to the Iliff School of Theology in Denver, Colorado.

Mary Kathryn taught English in public schools for nine years prior to answering the call to ministry. She holds a Bachelor of Science and a Master of Science in English and Political Science from Indiana State University and a Master of Divinity from the Iliff School of Theology.

Mary Kathryn enjoys searching for a rare piece of American Fostoria (glassware), nurturing flowers, and exploring God's global communities.

Born in Greensboro, North Carolina, Maxine West graduated from Bennett College with a degree in mathematics. She taught math and chemistry at Allen High School, Asheville, North Carolina, from 1963 until 1970, and was employed as a research chemist in the Asheville area for 15 years before joining the executive staff of the Women's Division, General Board of Global Ministries, The United Methodist Church in 1985.

With the Women's Division, Maxine served as executive secretary for organizational development and then assistant general secretary for resource management and marketing, with administrative responsibility for the Service Center and *Response* magazine.

Maxine retired on June 30, 2003, after 18 years of service. She still enjoys writing and researching the history of United Methodist Women and its predecessor organizations. She has taught in regional and conference Schools of Christian Mission.